Perspective on PROACTIVE Problem Solving

"Doug's joyful approach shows how to bring energy and fun to making things happen proactively. Can't change the past . . . can influence the future!"

—Doug Potter, *Eureka! Europe*

"When Doug meets Disney, creativity ne'er wanes. Our team explodes when he jump-starts our brains!"

—Ellen Guidera, VP, The Walt Disney Company

"I loved it. Selfishly, I can see it improving my non-business life for me and my family interactions. At 77, it is tough to find many self-improvement opportunities."

—Dave Kilbury, Retired Business Leader

"This is quite simply a brilliant book in its clarity, practical application, and easily digested examples. STOP STUPID. START SMART is a simple yet powerful thought. I have been applying the tenets of Doug's thinking for 25 years and it works, whether it's building billion dollar brands or helping you navigate your way around a nagging problem . . . A must-read!"

—Ken Grier, Founder of De-Still Creative Ltd.

"Doug provides understanding and guidance on the vital importance of stimulating joy in work by enabling employees to become part of the improvement of their work systems. He challenges us to stop stifling the natural motivations that fuel employee joy. When employees are engaged, a chain reaction of increased quality, efficiency, and productivity is sparked."

—Kevin E. Cahill, Executive Director,
The W. Edwards Deming Institute

"For anyone who leads teams, serves on teams, or wants their organization to perform at a high level, you need to read and truly digest PROACTIVE Problem Solving. *Innovation and working smart are the life blood of a successful business. And your greatest resources are your people at all levels and across all functions. Doug Hall's strategies, tools, and examples will help your business achieve more than you thought possible."*

—R. Bruce Montgomery Jr.,
Senior Operating Partner, Bourne Partners

"In PROACTIVE Problem Solving, *Doug Hall reminds us that the practices, opportunities, and solutions are different daily. He inspires us to continuously seek different and innovative ways to respond to our challenges and reach our goals. He draws from many life experiences and welcomes us on a journey to Sustaining Success with Never-Ending Improvement."*

—Rufus Glasper, PhD, President and CEO,
League for Innovation in the Community College

"Doug Hall has a great system for engineering innovation—that is, making it real—for meeting the often unrealized needs of an organization's external customers. Now Doug has turned those idea creation tools, methods, and psychology inward, applying them to internal organizational problems. Now, in this tightly written volume, he has made problem-solving even easier. Read it, study it, apply it, try any or all of the techniques, and prepare to be stunningly surprised at the results!"

—Barry J. Bruns, Col, USAF (Ret)

"At its core, Doug Hall's PROACTIVE Problem Solving *is about a better, faster way to turn brain matter into ideas. He gives you all sorts of ways to stimulate new thinking and ideas. Then he provides disciplined ways to sort those ideas, build on*

them, and turn them into practical actions that can improve the world, your world, and you."

—George Bradt, Founder of PrimeGenesis

"Only Doug Hall could make PROACTIVE Problem Solving *seem so effortless. Doug's energy for changing the world, one pioneer at a time, is admirable. His unwavering determination, and relentless pursuit to teach others how to make a meaningful difference, redefines what is possible. Thank you! Your innovation system has made an incredible difference in my life and in the lives of others."*

—Corinne Dupuy, Assistant Dean,
College of Engineering,
University of Louisiana at Lafayette

"People are generally really, really good at overcomplicating matters, and that makes common sense hard to find. In our non-profit organization, we can easily get lost day to day by being unfocused and inefficient if we do not break things down to their smallest parts to see them clearly. We have been blessed to have Doug steadfastly and patiently help us, nudge us, and guide us when we cannot see the trees for the forest. PROACTIVE Problem Solving *uses case studies to show how simple and effective problem-solving can be. It is a book I will re-read many times."*

—James MacHattie, Executive Director,
The College of Piping and Celtic Performing Arts of Canada

"This book is packed full of practical, relevant tools and insights that will help you deliver more effectively whatever your role, whatever your industry, for big complex projects and small problems alike."

—Graeme Crombie, Matrix, Scotland

"Doug Hall has done it again! His succinct approach to making problems real, using simple tools to explore the challenge and then 'experiencing the potential solutions' (yes with an S) that develops learning along the way, provides an awesome guide to achieve amazing outcomes!!!!"

—Lisa Henderson, Director of Client Services,
Vermont Manufacturing Extension Center

"PROACTIVE Problem Solving *takes you through the importance of a commitment to lifelong, never-ending learning. Doug uses his real world experiences to teach the principles of Defining Problems & Solutions, Creating Solutions, and Driving Out the Risks of Innovation. The result for his Brain Brew Distillery is one of the 12 best bourbons in America (Dexter) and the fastest growing super premium bourbon (Noble Oak). The book offers great insights on how to proactively solve problems. It also captures the daily challenges of business and ways to solve problems in a concise, employee-engaging, and fun manner."*

—Rick Rothwell, Systems Expert

"I've known Doug for over four decades, and his latest book is an excellent playbook that brings his considerable creative and engineering thinking to the masses. Employment empowerment is a huge challenge, and Doug has proven ways for your employees to become proactive problem solvers. In addition, there's plenty of pragmatic advice on how to define and solve challenging problems."

—Kip Knight, Founder, CMO Coaches

PROACTIVE Problem Solving

The Organizational Engagement System Behind the World's Most Disruptive Bourbon Distillery

Doug Hall

Dedicated with thanks and love to four amazing teams:
Eureka! Ranch
Innovation Engineering Institute
Brain Brew Distillery
Eureka! Europe

To paraphrase the Apple commercial:
Some Call Us the Crazy Ones . . .
And We're OK with that.

PROACTIVE Problem Solving

Published by Clerisy Press
Printed in the USA
Distributed by Publishers Group West
First edition, first printing

LCCN: 2024947195
ISBN: 978-1-57860-002-1 (hardcover); 978-1-57860-009-0 (ebook)

Eureka! Institute/Brain Brew Ventures
3849 Edwards Road, Cincinnati, Ohio 45244
513-271-9911
DougH@DougHall.com • EurekaRanch.com • BrainBrewWhiskey.com • BourbonFranchise.com

Clerisy Press
An imprint of AdventureKEEN
306 Greenup Street, Covington, KY 41011
800-678-7006; clerisypress.com

Table of Contents

Acknowledgments

IN WRITING THIS BOOK, I've come to the realization that my PRO-ACTIVE mindset was originally enabled by my parents and grandparents.

My mom, Jean Hall, knew I could create ideas before I did. She was my cheerleader.

My dad, Buzz Hall, was by my side, supporting me, when I embarked on creative adventures. He would encourage me to think before taking action and gently offer me ideas. When I failed, he would pick me up and get me going again. He never said, "I told you so." Rather, he would gently ask me what I had learned from my failure.

My grandmother, Hazel Hall, inspired, challenged, and pushed me to think big and bold. Her philosophy was made clear in an interview for my book *Making the Courage Connection* when she was age 88:

"You have to wind yourself up to find courage. It's easier to submit to whatever is. You have to shake yourself and say, "No, this isn't what I'm going to accept."

My great-grandfather Will Holder was the only entrepreneur in my family tree. As a sailmaker, he reinvented his business as the marketplace changed. As the age of sailing ended, he produced custom awnings and tarps. He was also an innovator of work systems. He was the first to bring a sewing machine into a Canadian sail loft. At age 95, he described his life philosophy with these simple words:

"One time you're down, another time you're up, then you're down again and you come up again."

Having family support was invaluable. In later years, many other mentors provided support. In particular, my girlfriend for 47 years and wife for 42 years, Debbie Hall, has provided support that is never-ending. When I was contemplating the creation of a distillery, I asked her advice. Without hesitation, she said, "Just do it!" Without her never-ending support there would be no Eureka! Ranch, Brain Brew Distillery, or Innovation Engineering Institute.

Introduction

An Antidote to the Multitude of Problems You Face

WE ARE LIVING IN A TIME OF UNPRECEDENTED CHANGE. The consequence is a never-ending stream of problems in our professional and personal lives. Concurrently, Gallup reports only 32% of employees are actively engaged. And the trend is negative. Eureka! Ranch research finds that 44% of managers feel employee engagement is worse since COVID.

The Eureka! Ranch study also found that the average manager wastes 3.5 hours a day reacting to flawed company work systems and employee mistakes. Interestingly, 78% of this waste is from flawed company work systems. These include poor work instructions, flawed digital systems, ineffective communications, and needless bureaucracy. Only 22% of wasted time is from employee mistakes.

The only effective way I've found to address this epidemic of waste is to engage the entire organization—employees, managers, and leadership—in proactively identifying and fixing the work system problems. I learned this as cofounder and CEO of the highly disruptive Brain Brew Bourbon Distillery. Despite the pandemic, by applying the lessons in this book to engage employees, Brain Brew grew from shipping a few thousand cases to shipping over 100,000 cases a year.

Stated simply, the complexity of today's world makes it nearly impossible for leaders to command and control their organizations. Rather, they need to engage and embrace the ideas, insights, and thinking of all their team members.

On June 24, 1980, a documentary broadcast by NBC told the story of how Dr. W. Edwards Deming, an American statistician, helped change the Japanese economy after WWII from a focus on low cost to high quality and reliability. Host Lloyd Dobyns had this to say about the need for broad-scale worker engagement:

> *In almost all the solutions to the problem of productivity there is a common thread. Each of them includes, in some way, worker participation. Every expert to whom we talked agreed that no solution can succeed fully unless it includes the active participation of the people who actually do the work, union or nonunion. All humans think, and nowhere is it chiseled in stone that those in management think best.*
>
> *If Japan Can, Why Can't We?*
> —NBC White Paper

My previous books, most recently *Driving Eureka!*, teach how to create and execute ideas for growing sales and profits through disruptive strategies, offerings, and business models.

This book is different. It's about helping YOU and those around you become PROACTIVE problem solvers. It's about teaching you how to move your mindset from "reactive" to embracing a more optimistic and proactive way of life.

The need for this book became real to me over the past few years as I experienced the thrills and challenges of leading what is arguably the world's most disruptive bourbon distillery. Leading the Brain Brew Distillery has taught me that while disruptive ideas for innovative products, services, and business models are critical, having a team of PROACTIVE problem solvers is just as important. If I were to break down relative importance, I would estimate that, when it comes to sustained success, 25% is due to having a disruptive product/service, 25% is a result of a disruptive business model, and fully 50% is because of never-ending continuous improvements by employees.

At Brain Brew, innovation by everyone, everywhere, every day is not optional. It is the job of every team member. From operations, to finance, to procurement, to marketing and sales, the Brain Brew Crew is on a never-ending quest to find smarter ways of working.

The distillery has the quirky name "Brain Brew" to remind team members that our collective mission is to work smarter than our competitors. Or, in the irreverent language of the Brain Brew Crew, our focus is to STOP THE STUPID.

By "stupid" we mean the stupid processes, work systems, and bureaucratic junk that develops within all organizations and industries. When Brain Brew was created, I had the preconception that we could create our production system once and be done with it. I was wrong. What I didn't understand was the need to reinvent our work systems as production grew from 600 to 10,000 to 24,000 to 48,000 to 70,000 to 100,000 cases. With each leap in production, work processes that had been SMART suddenly became STUPID. Dramatic growth impacted everything from raw material flow to work systems to production rhythm.

Joe Girgash, co-founder and president, quickly learned to think proactively about not just the current production increase but also the ones that will follow. He also engaged the team in the creation, testing, and implementation of system improvements. Just as the Walt Disney Company teaches employees to take immediate action to help frustrated guests, Joe taught the team to take action when they see something that is wrong. The impact of this cultural mindset is immense. In retrospect, committing to organizational engagement is one of the most important decisions we've made as a company.

Competing in the bourbon whiskey marketplace, we learned quickly that we would fail if we tried to follow the playbook of the multinational conglomerates that control 80% to 90% of bourbon whiskey sales. To win, we had to innovate our offerings, business models, and work systems to enable our "David" of a distillery to survive and thrive versus the "Goliaths" that dominate bourbon whiskey.

For the Brain Brew Crew, STOP THE STUPID means not accepting poor work methods, poor tools, or flawed work systems as being "just the way it is." When our team members SEE SOMETHING that is a problem, they are enabled to TRY SOMETHING to solve it. The result: Their work is more meaningful, and our distillery is more successful.

To be totally clear, STOP THE STUPID is about STUPID WORK **SYSTEMS,** NOT STUPID **PEOPLE!** People of all ages and education levels have insights and ideas. **There are no stupid people.** There are, however, many people who have not been taught how to problem-solve, validate, and communicate their ideas.

While the achievements of Brain Brew are amazing, the reality is we still have much to learn in our never-ending quest to work smarter than our competition. It is and always will be a never-ending journey of continuous improvement. Fortunately, we have laid the foundation of a culture that is ready, willing, and able to win.

Our sister company, the Eureka! Ranch, created a one-day PROACTIVE Problem Solving workshop for training employees at Brain Brew and other companies. The workshop adapted the Ranch's Innovation Engineering curriculum of courses and tools to focus on problem-solving instead of inventing "disruptive ideas" for growth strategies, offerings, or business models.

Unlike classic problem-solving courses that teach how to dissect a problem to find its cause, the workshop and this book teach how to look at each problem as a system of interconnected parts that are subjected to never-ending continuous improvement. To use a plumbing analogy, instead of teaching you how to "plug a leak," it teaches you how to create and execute ideas that vaporize the causes of the leak so that it never occurs again.

The PROACTIVE Problem Solving methods are easy to apply. And they work. An academic research study led by Dr. Andy

VanGundy of the University of Oklahoma found that these methods enable a 5X or 500% increase in the number of effective ideas for solutions created versus the methods most adults use. Having options for solutions increases your odds of success as you move from idea creation to implementation.

As you learn the PROACTIVE Problem Solving methods, you will develop confidence in your ability to proactively create a better future for yourself. And you will "future-proof" your success. Multiple studies find that thinking and problem-solving are among the top skills that employers look for in new employees. Recently, a research study of over 800 corporations published by the World Economic Forum quantified the need to future-proof your career. The study found that, over the next five years, employers expect to create 69 million new jobs. At the same time, they will eliminate 83 million positions. Yes, my friends—change is not optional.

An Invitation to Living a Life of Curiosity and Adventure

THIS BOOK IS MY INVITATION for you to take action on the adventure of improving the world around you. My goal is not to change you. In fact, if I tried to change you I would fail miserably. Rather, I invite you to embrace the intrinsic curiosity and wisdom that exists within you.

This book challenges you to let go of the comfortable relationships you've developed with problems. Instead of accepting life's frustrations as "just the way it is," stand up and use your brain to find a way to reduce and even vaporize your frustrations.

The process begins first and foremost by paying attention and living in the moment, mindful and curious. It involves experimentation and experiences that connect you to your sensory awareness, your curiosity, and your inherent quest for meaningfulness.

What's in it for Your Organization

IMAGINE WHAT IT WOULD BE LIKE if everyone across your culture was fully engaged. Imagine the impact on your efficiency and effectiveness if, like Japan Steel Works, each of your employees suggested and took action on 10 ideas per year! It would be transformative!

A major benefit of PROACTIVE Problem Solving is that it blends seamlessly with existing improvement systems such as Lean and Six Sigma. PROACTIVE Problem Solving turbocharges organizational engagement in problem-solving AND the organization's ability to create and execute Lean (ideas to increase value with less resources/waste) and Six Sigma (ideas to reduce process variation and enhance process control).

Business leaders tell us that the quick wins with Lean and Six Sigma tend to focus on addressing obvious waste and variation problems. They view PROACTIVE Problem Solving as a way to amplify their efforts to reduce waste and variation with ideas that are nonobvious.

The reason these three methodologies work together is because, at their root, they are all grounded in the teaching of Dr. W. Edwards Deming, who you will learn more about in the first chapter.

The two biggest benefits of full organizational engagement are:

1. A Chain Reaction of Business Impacts

Increasing organizational engagement activates a continuous stream of ideas for improved effectiveness, efficiency, capacity, safety, and quality, resulting in measurable impact. Tracking studies on students taking our training courses finds:

- Nearly 100% apply the new skills and mindset to their work.
- 60% can accomplish work they could not have done without the systems they learned.

- A company in Europe found that participants generated revenue growth or savings ranging from €300,000 to €6 million.

Research by the Gallup organization finds that organizations with high organizational engagement realize:

- 81% decrease in absenteeism
- 64% decrease in safety incidents/accidents
- 43% decrease in turnover for high-turnover organizations
- 42% decrease in quality defects
- 28% decrease in shrinkage/theft
- 18% decrease in turnover for low-turnover organizations

They also realize:

- 23% increase in profitability
- 18% increase in productivity/sales
- 10% increase in customer loyalty

2. Increased Job Satisfaction and Employee Retention

When employees feel their work has meaning, they are more engaged, and work is more fun. A Eureka! Ranch study involving 557 assessments across 122 companies found that the #1 predictor of employees feeling that their organization was one of the best places to work was, ***"My talents are well used in the workplace."***

The Secret to Employee Retention is SIMPLE: Educate and Enable Your Employees as PROACTIVE Problem Solvers!

WHEN EMPLOYEES HAVE AN OPPORTUNITY to use their brain, they feel an intrinsic reward. These intrinsic rewards are deep, sustainable, and meaningful. Conversely, when employees feel they are not listened to, they tune out, check out, and quit.

The Importance of Engaging Employees AND Managers

ENABLING BOTH EMPLOYEES AND MANAGERS is the key to success. However, research by the Eureka! Ranch finds that 74% of managers feel they don't have the training and support they need to problem-solve and help their employees. Interestingly, in a separate study we found that nearly the same percentage of managers (75%) find it difficult to get employees proactively engaged.

The need to support managers is also confirmed by *Training Magazine*'s annual survey. Their research finds that "Coaching/Developing Others" has been the #1 priority skill for leadership development for the past six years in a row.

This need to support managers is why at the end of each chapter there is a short section on "Insights for Managers of Proactive Employees." It's also why the Ranch team developed a course that helps teach managers the art and science of how to lead proactive employees.

The Foundation of This Book

THIS BOOK AND OUR PROACTIVE PROBLEM SOLVING workshop are grounded in a new field of academic study known as Innovation Engineering.

IE, as it's commonly called, was created by the Eureka! Ranch team in partnership with the University of Maine. It teaches students the art and science of innovation. It is taught by members of the Innovation Engineering Network at colleges, universities, and commercial training companies.

The full nine-course catalog is taught at universities as an undergraduate minor or as a graduate school certificate. It's also taught as an executive education course for managers and leaders of for-profit, nonprofit, and government organizations.

The curriculum is based on data from more than 20,000 real-world innovations plus quantitative research on innovation systems involving hundreds of thousands of adults. To date, Innovation Engineering organizations have developed and are developing innovation projects valued at over $20 billion.

This book translates the industrial-strength methods that I've relied on for 50-plus years to create BIG ideas into simple-to-learn and easy-to-implement principles for helping employees fix broken work systems and problem-solve ideas for working smarter.

PROACTIVE Problem Solving Versus Product/Service Innovation

WITH NEW PRODUCT/SERVICE INNOVATION there is often tremendous risk and complexity. Because of this new product/service innovation, teams follow a disciplined or even "formal" process that is documented and data driven.

PROACTIVE Problem Solving innovations are often developed and executed with less formality. As long as team leaders are engaged and have set appropriate boundaries, employees can very quickly identify a problem, create a solution, validate the solution, and publish their new way of working via changes to formal Standard Operating Procedures or through informal sharing across teammates or teams.

Less formality doesn't mean that ideas are necessarily less innovative. In fact, it's common that, when faced with problems where the answer isn't obvious, greater originality is required. Fortunately, the industrial-strength nature of Innovation Engineering methods enables employees to create ideas that are as big, bold, and unexpected as needed.

Informal will always be faster than formal. However, there still need to be checks and balances to make sure that new ideas don't have unintended consequences. At our distillery, we train our managers to evaluate and decide how informal or formal each project needs to be. We also have conversations about boundaries for which ideas are "just do them" and which ideas need to go through a more formal review process.

PROACTIVE Problem Solving Embodies and Supports the Mission

Adding PROACTIVE Problem Solving to the Innovation Engineering curriculum helps us accelerate achievement of our IE mission:

We exist to change the world
by helping everyone
work smarter and more innovatively together.

We do this through company customized
training and work systems.

- **Changing the World**—This bold statement energizes me. Quite simply, for myself and my teams, life is too short to not focus on making a meaningful impact on the world.
- **Company Customized**—It's not uncommon for training courses to contain an "implied criticism" of what employees are currently doing. This creates a barrier to learning. To avoid this we customize our training courses to celebrate examples of company employees creating and implementing ways to work smarter. Customization includes company success stories, plus alignment with the company's industry, language/lexicon, and existing training programs. Customizing the courses makes it easier for employees to "connect the dots" on how to apply the teachings to their existing work situation. The result is a bottom-up transformation of the organization's culture.

And that, my friends, is the reason why—after 50 years of innovating and now eight books—I have never been more excited to get up, get out, and get going each day!

Book Organization

Part One: DEFINING Problems and Solutions

The book begins with understanding WHAT your problem is and WHY it's important to solve it. This increases your odds of success by increasing focus and reducing wasted efforts. It also fuels your motivation to keep going with your problem-solving when first solutions hit "speed bumps."

Part Two: CREATING Solutions

Creating solutions involves the engagement and leadership of employees. This is the heart of the book. It is where you learn the most effective methods for creating solutions that I've found in 50 years of problem-solving. The methods are practical. They are also philosophical. They open new ways of looking at problems and solutions.

Part Three: Driving Out RISK as You Bring Your Idea to Life

Ideas are good. Making ideas real is great. The final part of the book outlines a reliable system for concurrently decreasing risk and increasing success with your solutions. Having a disciplined system for exploring, testing, and learning about new ideas builds problem-solving courage. Students tell us that when they understand HOW they can easily learn more about the potential for their ideas, they are more comfortable suggesting and pursuing new ideas.

In this book I also explore the basic psychology behind what makes a method work or not work. I'm not a psychologist, so it won't be a ponderous discussion. That said, I have learned that, when it comes to creating ideas, the greatest barriers are psychological.

My appreciation for psychology came from writing the first ever chapter on innovation for the American Psychological Association's

Handbook of Consumer Psychology. Writing the chapter forced me to think deeply about the links between creativity and psychology.

Examples of How Students Have Used This Learning

Here's a random sample of problem-solving projects that IE students have led. The projects cover a broad range of industries, departments, and job levels.

- How to decrease the time it takes from awarding a project to the suppliers getting the necessary materials.
- How to enable two departments to work together more effectively to increase productivity and quality.
- Creating an on-site garden to reuse materials and help demonstrate a commitment toward sustainability.
- Creating novel learning experiences for teachers, to inspire change in instructional practices.
- Reinventing onboarding training.
- Innovative curriculum design and development to meet changing industry demand.
- A new framework for team meetings when problem-solving or decision-making is needed.
- Expanding capacity for an existing product line.
- A system to provide real-time inventory and order tracking as they scale up.
- Scaling up an experimental process while reducing risk with the process.
- How to reduce downtime, standardize work, and enable automation.
- How to harvest and house energy for sensing technology.
- New application methods to enable faster product launches.
- More effectively getting food donations to members in need before it expires.
- Ideas for a new post-op scheduling system.
- Teaching students how to earn and utilize money in an age-appropriate way that also grows with them.
- Enabling disabled students to be more independent.

- New methods for identifying, recruiting, and retaining high-quality sales agents.
- How to reduce scrap material at a mill.
- Methods for sharing information between internal sub-categories.
- Reducing time needed for GED completion.
- Cutting the time needed to complete a design review with suppliers by 25–50%.
- How to collect stories to share with the public from all voices and departments within their organization.
- Methods to reduce delays during new product development with suppliers.
- New ways to notify personnel about pending tasks to reduce time to completion.
- Creating a program to successfully establish a patent portfolio.
- More effective ways to operate as one powerful team.

Confidentiality

In this book I tell stories about the creation of ideas. Every story is true to the best of my recollection. However, the bulk of my work over the years is covered by confidentiality agreements. Therefore, in many cases I've disguised the names of people, organizations, and sometimes even the industry when it might be easy to guess who I am talking about.

"Idea Guru?"

A May 2000 *Inc. Magazine* cover story dubbed me "The Idea Guru." The term has since been used many times by reporters to describe me.

I've never really liked the term "guru" because it implies that idea creation is mystical magic. And, frankly, my life's work is to make the creative process reliable and reproducible—not mystical. However, when I looked up the definition of "guru" in the Merriam-Webster dictionary, I became more comfortable with it. It defined a guru as "a person with knowledge or expertise."

I also find "idea guru" better than what NFL players called me when I ran a course teaching them how to think smarter about their entrepreneurial investments. At the end of day two, a retired lineman, standing over a foot taller than I, with multiple Super Bowl Rings, said, "Doug, you are the OG." Other players heard him and yelled out "Yeah, the OG." They then raised their glasses of our Noble Oak Bourbon in a toast. Now I understand that calling me an OG—"Original Gangster" is a major compliment—but to me it's a bit weird. I think I'll stick with being an IG instead of an OG.

In closing, I'd like to give special thanks to Patty Giavara, who provided wise and helpful feedback on version after version of this book, and to Lydia Carson for her amazing editing of the final draft. Also thanks to Graeme Crombie, Maggie Pfeifer, Rick Rothwell, Barry Bruns, Ron Walters, and Bruce Montgomery for their insights and ideas. The book is much better because of their wisdom.

Enjoy the adventure!

Cheers, Doug
DougH@EurekaRanch.com
Springbrook, PEI, Canada
Cincinnati, Ohio, USA

PART ONE

DEFINING Problems and Solutions

1. THE FOUNDATION
2. PROACTIVELY IDENTIFYING THE WHAT AND WHY OF PROBLEMS
3. COMMUNICATING SOLUTIONS AND ENROLLING OTHERS

CHAPTER 1

The Foundation

THERE ARE FEW THINGS MORE FRUSTRATING than to face STUPIDITY in your personal and professional life. In the context of this book, STUPIDITY ranges from poorly designed forms that are not clear; to work systems that create more rework than productive work; to tasks that are not achievable with current skills, tools, and work systems.

A "stupid" work system is one that is obviously flawed. It causes frustration implementing it, regular errors, regular rework, and/or extra work. It is also reliable. There is a high certainty that it will recur repeatedly.

Inside most organizations, many problems are judged to not be "stupid enough" to invest time and energy to fix them. The belief is that the organization's limited, centralized problem-solving resources need to be invested on "bigger" problems.

Limitations on centralized resources are a very real constraint. PROACTIVE Problem Solving addresses this limitation by engaging employees in solving problems. To accomplish this they require training, tools, and, most importantly, coaching on problem-solving.

Ideally, the process starts with an employee speaking up about a problem that they have observed. Sadly, many adults don't speak up about problems, often because they don't have confidence in their problem-solving skills, or they have never been told that problem-solving is part of their responsibility. As a result, when they see something, they say and do nothing.

Another challenge is when employees feel that bringing up a problem without a solution will make them look stupid. This is such a big problem that the *Harvard Business Review* published an article on it in its February 2008 edition, "Don't Bring Me Problems—Bring Me Solutions!" The article quotes Frances Frei, a Harvard Business School professor:

> *Sending out this message (Don't bring me problems—bring me solutions!) doesn't work. Instead of promoting accountability, it encourages employees to turn a blind eye to problems they see but cannot figure out how to fix. When you say, "Don't bring me problems—bring me solutions," what you're saying, in effect, is "Of all the problems you find, I only want to know about the ones you can solve."*
>
> *Identifying problems can be a solo sport, but finding solutions rarely is. This is especially true when the problems have any degree of complexity. If you're giving people permission to tell you about just those problems they can solve, you're missing out on many opportunities for improvement. You're leaving performance boosters on the table simply because the problem and the solution aren't collocated.*

The goal of PROACTIVE Problem Solving is to enable employees to take action by teaching them a system for thinking smarter, faster, and more creatively. We define proactive as: Creating or controlling a situation by causing something to happen rather than responding to it after it has happened.

In simple terms, it means "When You See Something, Say or Do Something."

PROACTIVE Problem Solving is when you voluntarily make a change that improves your work situation or life. It can be an idea that helps you work smarter, more efficiently, more effectively, more safely, and so on. PROACTIVE Problem Solving examples include when a nurse finds a way to reduce patient wait time or when a manufacturing employee finds a way to reduce rework, or a customer service rep discovers a way to increase customer satisfaction.

"Reactive" problem-solving is about addressing a problem that has suddenly appeared. The goal is to get things "back on track" as soon as possible. Reactive problem-solving examples include when an existing system—such as production, customer service, or an operational system—breaks down. Other "reactive" situations include when forces outside of your control occur, such as economic changes or new competitors, or even when bad weather suddenly appears during an outdoor event.

Many Kinds of Problems to Be Solved

This book can help you with reactive problems, but even more importantly, it can help you identify and address problems proactively that are not demanding solutions.

Many problems can appear to be small and unimportant. However, we've found that little problems can grow into big problems. They also can cause frustrations that steal "joy of work" from employees, fueling a negative attitude that reduces engagement.

Examples of these problems include:

- Small problems that REPEAT REGULARLY.
- Small problems that could GROW BIG.
- Problems that WASTE TIME/MONEY.

Addressing such challenges builds your problem-solving capability. As your confidence in your ability to create solutions grows, you will soon take on bigger problems in both your work and personal life. The result is that you live a life filled with curiosity and hope for the future.

Documenting PROACTIVE Problem Solving Success

In a work setting, the solutions you create can be implemented and shared with others either formally or informally.

The formal approach involves making changes to your organization's SOP or Standard Operating Procedure. These include the training, instructions, checklists, and systems used to help employees work smarter, faster, and more cost efficiently.

Documenting validated changes to a formal SOP is the most reliable way to grow the success of your organization.

However, many organizations have not yet embraced SOP documentation of their best work practices. Instead, new work systems are shared informally from employee to employee. This approach is helpful but can be unreliable.

When making formal changes to your work process it's important that you have a system for reviewing and approving changes to make sure that a proposed idea doesn't have unintended consequences for other parts of the organization.

Documentation also makes it easy to quantify the impact of your PROACTIVE Problem Solving culture, as you can easily count the number of improvements to your work systems.

94% of the Problem Is the System—6% Is the Employee

One of my greatest pet peeves is when people are blamed for a mistake that is out of their control. It is unfair to blame someone for a failure when they've not been provided the training, tools, or a reliable system for doing the task asked of them.

A foundation of this book and Innovation Engineering is the system-thinking mindset of Dr. W. Edward Deming. He is famous for:

1) Helping the Allies win World War II through the production of more reliable military equipment.
2) Helping Japan rebuild its economy after the war with a focus on quality (most famously at Toyota).
3) Teaching the Western world in the early 1980s how to create quality and never-ending improvement. His work is the foundation of such programs as Lean, Six Sigma, and Innovation Engineering.

I learned about Dr. Deming from my father, M. Bradford Hall, who worked with him at Nashua Corporation, the first US company to embrace Dr. Deming's teachings. When I was studying chemical engineering, my father insisted that I learn the Deming mindset. Over and over he would remind me that, as Dr. Deming taught:

94% of failures are due to the system. 6% are due to the worker.

Dr. Deming defined a *system* as a set of interconnected parts that work together to accomplish a common aim.

Instead of blaming employees when failure occurs, he encouraged managers to think deeper. He taught that most problems are "common cause." They are built into the system, the work process, tools, training, raw materials, and so on. He also taught that worker-caused or "special cause" problems are rare. He believed that humans wanted to do quality work, but poor systems robbed them of them of the ability to perform well.

When asked how he would summarize his life's work in a few words, he said: "I would say it has to do with Pride of Work."

Sadly, a Eureka! Ranch survey of more than 12,000 employees finds that, today, only 5% have high "pride of work."

STOP.

THINK.

Read this again. In a survey of more than 12,000 employees, only 5% have high "pride of work." Very frustrating. It's also why I am so passionate about teaching and activating PROACTIVE Problem Solving!

Dr. Deming also taught the importance of leaders and workers being proactive in taking responsibility for the systems that make up our work cultures. He wrote:

> *The aim of leadership should be to improve the performance of employees, to improve quality, to increase output, and simultaneously to bring pride of workmanship to people. Put in a negative way, the aim of leadership is not merely to find and record failures of employees, but to remove the causes of failure: to help people to do a better job with less effort.*

From 1950 to 1962, the application of system thinking across Japanese industry was led by teams of experts. In 1962, that changed when Sumitomo Electric won the Deming Prize (the national prize for manufacturing quality is named in honor of Dr. Deming for his contribution to rebuilding Japan).

What made Sumitomo's win unique was that it was the first company to win using "participatory management." Employees were taught, coached, and enabled to be proactive problem solvers. This approach was soon adopted across Japanese industry. Kenneth Hopper, author of

The Puritan Gift, shared the Sumitomo story with me. He also showed me data on how, by broadly adopting participatory management, Japan grew its economy some 300% faster than the US and UK over the following 15 years.

Productivity Gains Evidenced by Deming's Teachings

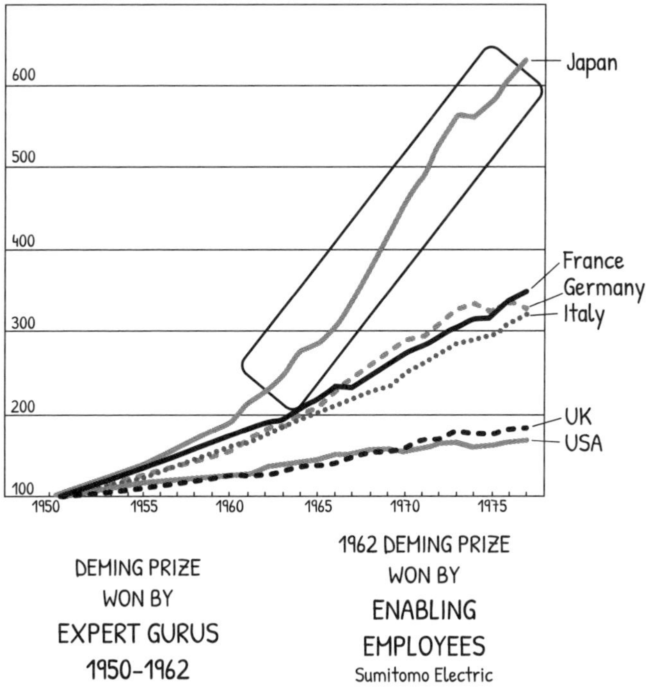

On June 24, 1980, NBC televised a documentary *If Japan Can, Why Can't We?* produced by Clare Crawford-Mason. It introduced Dr. Deming to the Western world. It also featured the results of a project on carbonless paper production led by my father, with coaching support by Dr. Deming, that showed how millions of dollars could be saved through the adoption of system thinking.

System Thinking from 1) Manufacturing to 2) Innovation to 3) Igniting Organizational Engagement

From 1950 to 1990, the application of Dr. Deming's system thinking was focused on improving manufacturing quality, capacity, and costs, as these were the greatest challenges for companies.

From 1990 to 2020, the Eureka! Ranch team focused on applying Deming's system thinking to product and services innovations that help companies increase sales and profit margins. This was and is successful with innovation thought leaders such as Walt Disney, Nike, American Express, Procter & Gamble, Hewlett Packard, Pepsi-Cola, AT&T, and thousands of other industrial, service, nonprofit, and government organizations.

Today, the primary challenge facing organizations is engagement. To address this, Deming's teachings are being applied to ignite organizational engagement in fixing problems and finding ideas for working smarter.

How to Identify if a Solution is Worth the Investment of Your Time

To enable participatory management, there must be a common standard for deciding if an idea justifies spending time and energy on it. Forty years of quantitative research by the Eureka! Ranch team, involving tens of thousands of ideas and hundreds of marketplace validations, found that successful ideas are MEANINGFULLY UNIQUE.

MEANINGFUL: A change with high potential to make a tangible impact. An idea that offers the potential for making a genuine improvement.

UNIQUE: A real change in our systems or how we work. Something we are not doing now.

The Meaningfully Unique definition focuses our energy on ideas with the potential to make a real and positive difference.

Without the Meaningfully Unique standard, it can be easy to fool ourselves into believing that we can resolve a problem:

- By working harder using the same methods.
- By pushing workers to simply "make fewer mistakes."
- By ignoring the problem in hopes it will evaporate by itself.

A Simple Example of Meaningful Uniqueness

The career counseling department at a midsize urban college found it very difficult to get students to visit their office. The consequence was that many students were not getting the help they needed to prepare for entering the job market.

After attempts at emailing and texting failed to connect with students, the team decided to try something different. They set up a table in the student parking garage in the morning and afternoon—when students were coming and going—to make connections with students.

The disruptive idea of a college department working in a parking garage created a new momentum towards career counseling. Students taking advantage of counseling dramatically increased.

Connecting with students in their campus parking garage was a meaningful and unique idea. It transformed the success of the career counseling service.

Creating a Craft Bourbon Distillery

Creating a bourbon distillery is very, very expensive if you are successful. That's because of the massive capital investment required to make and age bourbon barrels for six to eight years.

The bourbon distillery was sparked by a curiosity to find a way to not have to wait for years to create world-class bourbon whiskey. The starting insight was the industry belief that 70% to 80% of the flavor of whiskey comes from the interaction between the bourbon and the wood of whiskey barrels. This interaction reminded me of my experiences as a young chemical engineer at the Procter & Gamble pulp mill in Mehoopany, Pennsylvania.

In simple terms, when you make paper, you use heat to remove the lignins, a polymer, from the cellulose. When you make whiskey, you use heating and cooling (morning to night, summer to winter) to develop the whiskey flavor and color. When it is warm, the whiskey goes through the char of the inside of the barrel and into the wood. The whiskey then bonds with the lignins and, as the barrel gets cold, they are extracted into the barrel. This interaction of wood with whiskey caused by heating and cooling sets off chemical reactions that create luxury smoothness, flavor, and color.

Controlling the interaction of wood and whiskey is not simple and, interestingly, is not linear. Never-ending curiosity led cofounder Joe Girgash and me to conduct over 3,000 experiments and hundreds of quantitative paired-comparison blind tests against the world's top bourbons. This is how we discovered the process we named Wood-Craft Finishing.

After 18 months, we knew we were onto something when our bourbons won two of eight double gold medals at the North American Whiskey championship. The products were so amazing we were able to convince Edrington (makers of The Macallan, the world's most expensive whiskey) to collaborate with us. The result of our joint venture is Noble Oak Double Oak Bourbon and Rye. They have won top scores of 95 and 97 points in competitions. Today, the brand is in national distribution across the US, the fastest growing super premium bourbon brand in America.

Separate from our collaboration with Edrington, we created Dexter Three Wood Bourbon. It was a pandemic project focused on creating a true ultra-premium luxury bourbon. Following the systems taught in this book, we continually improved it till it was named as one of the 12 best bourbons in the world at the prestigious Ultimate Spirits Challenge.

A major benefit of WoodCraft finishing is that it allows us to age the bourbon for much less time. Our CFO has calculated that if we were not using WoodCraft we would have needed about $30 million in additional capital investment to fund barrel aging to get to our current 100,000 cases of production a year.

Insights for Managers of Proactive Employees

1. GREAT MANAGERS BELIEVE IN THE GOODNESS OF ALL PEOPLE: Fundamental to being a great leader of proactive employees is an unshakable belief that your people are fundamentally good. It's about believing that everyone wants to do great things. My father learned this from Dr. Deming. In a talk my father gave on Deming at a paper industry convention, he said:

> *The problem is not the workers. What we have proven at Nashua and what anyone can prove if they enter this way of thinking is that the majority of the workers anywhere in the world will perform well if given the tools and proper support of management.*

Managers who believe in the goodness of their team generate amazing results. Those who don't believe end up with a never-ending revolving staff as folks leave or are fired as they don't become engaged. Believing in your people means taking responsibility for continually improving their training, tools, and work systems.

2. SETTING BOUNDARIES: As the manager, you have a broader view of the organization than your employees. You also understand the interconnections between your work and the work of others. A key part of your job is to educate employees on the boundaries and organizational constraints that exist. Without an understanding of boundaries, it is likely that your employees will end up wasting time on changes that fail because of issues they were not aware of. The good news is that, as you educate them about how their work impacts others, they quickly become even more effective PROACTIVE Problem Solvers.

3. DON'T PENALIZE THE PROBLEM FINDER: As you activate problem-solving within your team, it is easy to fall back to a mindset of penalizing problem finders by telling them "you found it, you fix it." Done repeatedly, this message will result in employees not bringing up problems. The alternative approach is for you to genuinely thank them for identifying the problem and ask if they want to work to solve it. If they do, take the time to teach, coach, and support their problem-solving. The first time you go through this process, it will require a significant investment of time. However, as team members gain confidence in their problem-solving, they will be able to do it with less and less of your time. This "force multiplier" enables you and your team to do more.

4. QUANTIFYING MEANINGFUL UNIQUENESS: Ideas that offer Meaningful Uniqueness have greater odds of success. In fact, it's one of the most predictive measures of success. With problem-solving, it's often easy to determine if an idea is Meaningful (has reasonable odds of having a positive impact) and Unique (something we're not doing and/or haven't tried).

There are times, however, when there are many options for how to address a problem with no clear "best" idea. In these cases, it is useful to quantify the opinions of those who are knowledgeable about the situation. At the Eureka! Ranch we measure opinions using an automated survey tool that measures Meaningfulness of each idea, based on how much they "like the idea" and Uniqueness based on how "new and different" they feel each idea is. Opinions are gathered using a 0-to-10 scale. The results are weighted 60% Meaningfulness and 40% Uniqueness for an overall Meaningful Uniqueness Rating. Importantly, the data is not a replacement for your management judgment. Rather, it is an input and aid to helping you make smarter decisions.

CHAPTER 2

Proactively Identifying the What and Why of Problems

LIKE MANY PEOPLE, you may not think of yourself as an "idea" person. But suddenly you find yourself so frustrated with a recurring problem that you just can't deal with it anymore. Your mind is activated to find a way to solve it.

After some work, you think of a solution. Your new approach is so exciting you can hardly stop thinking about it. You can clearly see the benefits that your idea can deliver for you and your organization. And so you begin the adventure of turning your idea into reality.

All is going well with implementation, then UGH! You hit an unforeseen barrier to your idea. In the language of Innovation Engineering, we label this barrier a "Death Threat" to the development of your idea. The term "Death Threat" gives emotional magnitude to the barrier.

If you're not careful, within minutes of hitting a major Death Threat, you start to second-guess your idea. Your old doubts and fears of problem-solving consume you. Your logical brain starts to squash your idea—"I told you it would never work," you tell yourself. You start thinking maybe you should give up. Maybe you should go back to accepting the problem as unavoidable.

For those with confidence in their problem-solving capability, the scenario is different. When the Death Threat is identified, they, too, hear the whispering in their brain to give up. However, these people neutralize the negatives with the power of purpose. They return to the WHAT and WHY of their project.

They reflect on the broader purpose of WHAT they are trying to accomplish. And, most important of all, WHY it matters. From the WHY, they gain the energy to pick themselves up and start again. They then use their problem-solving skills to address the Death Threat. In a short time, they create an idea for vaporizing the Death Threat and are soon back on track, implementing their new idea.

The difference between giving up and finding a way comes down to two things:

1) Your confidence in your ability to find a solution to the Death Threat.
2) The intrinsic motivation you feel for WHY this problem is very important to solve.

Intrinsic motivation is fueled by your personal frustration and the empathy you feel for others who face the same problem. It's also driven by your belief in the rightness of your mission to make your problem go away!

Together, your confidence and intrinsic motivation keep you going when others quit. You can call the intrinsic motivation whatever you want—mission, purpose, pride, the "why." In the end they are just different ways of finding meaning from your work.

Getting Started with PROACTIVE Problem Solving

Getting started with PROACTIVE Problem Solving requires you to let go of existing work patterns and methods. This can be difficult for some people. As author David DiSalvo explained in *What Makes Your Brain Happy and Why You Should Do the Opposite:* "The brain lives on a preferred diet of stability, certainty, and consistency, and it perceives unpredictability, uncertainty, and instability as threats to its survival."

Building your comfort with the uncertainty, you may feel that when you speak up about something you see as STUPID, it takes time. An easy way to start is by simply stopping and consciously noticing when you encounter something STUPID. When you see something, just say to yourself, "That's stupid." Then go on with your day. As time goes on, your acceptance of STUPID will decline. Within you will grow the natural human desire to STOP Stupid and to START doing things smarter.

Starting with Stop Stupid provides you with personal reward and motivation to change. Having removed some of your personal pains and frustrations, the next step in your Proactive development is to engage on team projects. Your team leader/manager has problems of a broader scope that you can help solve. Lastly, your confidence and capability to solve personal and team challenges prepares you to help your business unit or company leadership execute disruptive innovations. Disruptive innovations are ideas for new or improved products or services that can help the company increase sales and profitability versus competition. The challenge with truly disruptive ideas is they also require changes and adjustments by multiple company departments to make them feasible.

Taking Action Even When You Don't Feel Pain

It's easier to take action when you feel pain from a broken work system, process, or piece of equipment. The pain you feel ignites a desire for you to create a solution.

It's more difficult to ignite change when pain is low. Instead, we suffer with the flawed system as being "just the way it is."

In most cultures, management teaches that resources should be focused on only the biggest problems. In fact, the strategic planning process at its foundation is about focusing energy on the "biggest" opportunities for growth or improvement.

Frontline employees soon learn that the problems they face daily are not the type that management is interested in fixing. As a result, they stop reporting their problems and frustrations and learn to live with them.

With PROACTIVE Problem Solving, employees, managers, and middle managers are enabled and empowered to fix even the smallest of problems. They are unleashed to find and take action on ideas for working smarter—or, said another way, to "do the right thing."

The Start of PROACTIVE Problem Solving

To begin the process, ask yourself some questions.

WHAT is a challenge I want to evaporate? Summarize the problem in a way that makes it easy for others to understand.

WHAT is a recurring/frequent problem? These are problems that we know with high certainty will repeat. They are "reliable" frustrations in your life. They can be a small "speed bump" in how you work. They can be the problem that you've had to fix 234 times, and you have now decided that enough is enough.

Reliable recurring problems might not seem worth the effort to fix. However, doing the math can change your perspective. Consider that a small problem that wastes just 20 minutes every other day for two people in your organization results in 86 hours of wasted time a year!

WHAT is a big problem that happens infrequently? These are problems that are rare but devastating when they occur. Examples include systems that are vulnerable to causing a shutdown of your software system, a product recall, a serious worker accident, or a mistake that could do serious damage to your organization's reputation.

Why is the Energy Source for PROACTIVE Problem Solving

Problem-solving takes work. Implementing solutions takes energy.

The most effective energy source for powering change is understanding WHY the problem is very important. Understanding WHY creates intrinsic energy within you to solve it. It also often creates "pull" from the organization to realize the benefits that come from solving a problem.

WHY gives you the courage to think differently. It focuses your energy on the achievement of your mission. Your commitment to fixing the problem opens your mind to bigger and bolder ideas.

WHY is powered by your VALUES on what is right. Projects that align with your sense of how things "should be" versus "what is now" ignite personal energy. Your desire for the end result pulls you past naysayers and doubters.

WHY is powered by COMMON SENSE. When a work system is flawed, you know it. It's not something that requires great amounts of research. Stupid is stupid.

WHY is powered by SIMPLE MATH. Doing the math to quantify the impact that could be realized from solving a problem is motivational. However, doing math on something that is a new idea can be challenging. Fortunately, there is a system for quantifying the impact of your new ideas. In chapter 10 you will learn that system.

What and Why Are the Heart of Commander's Intent

To provide direction to problem-solving and disruptive innovation initiatives, the Eureka! Ranch has developed a variation of the planning approach that most military leaders use called Commander's Intent.

Chad Storlie described Commander's Intent in an article for *Harvard Business Review* this way:

> *How does your team respond when a plan changes? Does everyone seem to know what to do or is there confusion, a lack of meaningful activity, or people standing around waiting to be told what to do next? Planning is difficult whether in business or the military. Military planners use Commander's Intent, a key element to help a plan maintain relevancy and applicability in a chaotic, dynamic, and resource-constrained environment.*
>
> *Commander's Intent describes how the Commander (read: CEO) envisions the battlefield at the conclusion of the mission. It shows what success looks like. Commander's Intent fully recognizes the chaos, lack of a complete information picture, changes in enemy situation, and other relevant factors that may make a plan either completely or partially obsolete when it is executed. The role of Commander's Intent is to empower subordinates and guide their initiative and improvisation as they adapt the plan to the changed battlefield environment.*

We begin PROACTIVE Problem Solving by articulating WHAT and WHY in a short "Problem Statement" that summarizes the situation being addressed. Here are a few examples:

A Cross-Department Challenge

> *10% of customer orders placed by our field sales teams have significant mistakes each month. This causes us to waste time*

calling and emailing to correct them. Worse, when we miss the mistakes, they get sent to operations who ship the wrong things. We need ideas for helping our sales team get the orders right at the start.

A Simple Worker Problem

Clean up after private events at our facility takes on average 1.5 hours each night. This costs us money and it is not great for team morale when you don't get home till midnight. We need ideas for systems that we could use to cut the time it takes to clean up by at least 50%.

A Rework Problem

Our offerings are very complex. As a result, we have many specialists who work on them. The problem is that work by a specialist in one area causes problems for another area. To make it worse, we often don't find these interaction problems till late in the development process. This causes huge delays because of the need for rework and is also demoralizing for the team. We need ideas for improving information sharing between our specialist developers in order to prevent rework.

Make your WHAT and WHY as clear and easy to understand as possible. Your goal is to make it nearly impossible to NOT understand the problem and why you need ideas to address it.

Problem Statements often stand by themselves because of the clarity of the WHAT and WHY. To make sure you are very clear, it is often helpful to end the statement with a summary of the challenge in a sentence. This ending sentence often begins with "We need ideas for. . . ." It focuses everyone's thinking on the precise types of solutions you are looking for.

Summarize Your Problem

Problem Statements are a clear articulation of the situation you face and the consequences it causes.

Writing them requires you to think deeply about the problem.

The Innovation Engineering community of innovators around the world have found that freewriting is the most effective way to quickly think deeper about a problem. It's a simple process of writing about your challenge on a piece of paper or a keyboard. It involves simply writing down the thoughts in your head, then organizing those thoughts into a clear Problem Statement.

Here are some prompts that can help you get started with defining the WHAT and WHY of your problem.

PROMPTS for WHAT problem you should work on:

1. WHAT problems are SMALL but happen regularly?
2. WHAT problems are BIG and infrequent yet DEVASTATING?
3. WHAT things should we PREVENT before they become bigger issues?
4. WHAT problems exist that you can PREDICT will occur?
5. WHAT problems do you notice that most other people miss?
6. In five words or less, we need ideas for . . .
7. If I could wave a "magic wand," then the problem I would make disappear is . . .

Here are some prompts for helping you write about an existing problem.

PROMPTS for helping define WHAT the problem is:

1. WHAT is different versus the ideal?
2. What IS working and what IS NOT working?
3. What could be or might be the root cause of the problem?

4. What is not obvious about the problem that others might miss?
5. What is the REAL problem you are facing?
5. In five words or less, we need ideas for . . .

PROMPTS for WHY it's important to solve the problem now:

1. DEFINE why you think it is important to solve this problem.
2. DEFINE the benefits of solving this problem.
3. DEFINE the possible consequences of not solving this problem.

After writing your thoughts on paper, take a fresh sheet of paper or computer screen and write your Problem Statement.

PROMPTS for Problem Statements:

1. The problem we face is . . .
2. This is important to solve because . . .
3. We need ideas for . . .

To ensure clarity of your Problem Statement, read it out loud with a full voice. We've learned from experience that hearing an idea is different from reading an idea.

Blue Cards—A System for Summarizing Complex Challenges

A simple "Problem Statement" paragraph works for the vast majority of problems you will face.

When the problem is very complex or when multiple people will be working on it, we use a system called Blue Cards. A classic Blue Card includes:

Narrative: This is an expanded version of your Problem Statement. It explains your challenge so that the stakeholders involved in the problem area can clearly understand what the problem is and why it's important.

Mission: This is a tight articulation of what kind of ideas you are looking for.

Strategic Exclusions: These are the types of ideas you are NOT looking for as part of this problem-solving. They can be strategic or operational areas you don't want to consider at this time.

Tactical Constraints: These are executional boundaries and requirements. They often include constraints on money, time, and/or resources. They can also include regulations to be followed or tactical "musts" or "must nots."

Exploration Areas: This is an optional section designed to help bring the rest of the Blue Card to life for the reader. Done correctly, notes here can help accelerate the start of the project by identifying areas to look for potential solutions and/or people who might be helpful in finding a solution.

How a Blue Card Inspired a State Unemployment Agency

Innovation Engineering Black Belt Rick Rothwell shared a story of how clarity of mission helped a state unemployment agency.

The economy in this state was struggling. An economic downturn resulted in dramatic increases in unemployment claims. The agency responsible for helping the unemployed had flawed work systems. The Claims Center staff worked hard but not effectively. The average hold time to speak to a claims center person was about 20 minutes, with some hold times approaching 2 1/2 hours. The number of abandoned calls was huge—almost half of the callers hung up before their calls were answered.

Leadership within the agency did not know how to respond to the huge increase in workload. Andy Losasso was hired to lead the call center. He had been through some Innovation Engineering training and was informally coached by Rick. Andy began exploring ways to identify and solve the Claims Center's problems. Rather than accepting the poor performance, he sought a more proactive approach.

He fully understood that "94% of the problems are due to the systems." Realizing that the process for handling calls was not effective at all, he engaged the claims center staff members who were closest to the work.

The Blue Card WHAT was responsiveness —answering the phones in a timely manner. The WHY was to deliver on the agency's banner value—efficient customer service for our citizens in their time of need.

Several experiments were run over the next several weeks, using the Plan-Do-Study-Act (PDSA) learning cycle methodology. It's an iterative process where you start with a Plan—a hypothesis of how you might solve your problem, Then you Do something to test your hypothesis. Next, you Study why the test worked or didn't work. Lastly, you Act on your learning—adopting the change, archiving it, or, most commonly, you develop another hypothesis and repeat the Plan-Do-Study-Act process. PDSA is described in greater detail in chapter 9.

The PDSA process created organizational engagement across the team. Working together, they divided unemployment calls into "two lanes." Lane 1 handled easier, more basic questions that junior people could answer. Lane 2 handled the harder, more detailed questions and situations that required more senior people and took longer. This simple change in the systems led to dramatic improvements.

Andy also found that the telephone system already in use offered the technology necessary to implement improvements. By collaborating with the telephone system provider, the agency was able to fully take advantage of this existing technology resource.

Immediately, the hold times started to drop, and more calls were answered in a timely manner. As the hold times reduced, the Claims Center people didn't have to apologize to the callers and endure their disappointment for the long hold times. It is hard to feel that you are making a meaningful difference when you must apologize to almost every caller for the hold times—or get chewed out by them. Employees' pride in their work was restored.

During the same period a year later, with an increase of 7,000 calls over the same period, the hold times and abandoned calls had dropped significantly. The abandoned calls went from almost 50% to 15%. The average hold times declined from 20 minutes to 5 minutes, during the busiest period.

Most amazingly, all the improvements came at NO COST to the agency. No purchase of equipment or programming support was made, and no additional people were hired. The improvements were made to the systems through engagement of the frontline call center staff and better use of already available technology.

Looking back, Andy said, "The biggest lesson of this project was that people want to do a good job. Nobody desires to be bad at what they do, and because of that, people take pride in their work. They take pride even when their leadership has asked them, even with the best of intentions, to do the wrong things. A change in how people do their jobs needs to start with the systems and the tools that are in place. Without proper support, users become a part of flawed systems and unwittingly support them. The Claims Center agents were victims of the process just as much as the callers. By addressing the system and not the people, and by offering transparency and inclusion along the way, the agents took ownership of the changes and helped to push the changes forward."

Inventing a System for Increasing Profitability

The success of our Noble Oak and Dexter Bourbons was very exciting. However, given the complexities of the system of distributors, brokers, and retailers, there was always pressure on our profitability.

We developed a Brain Brew Bourbon Distillery Blue Card to discover a pathway to higher profitability. Ideas were explored. Some were prototyped and even shared with potential customers.

The answer to our quest came from exploring the history of bourbon and American whiskey. From our research, we learned that, in the 1800s, 85% of American whiskey came from Cincinnati. It was at the time the sixth-largest city in the country.

Interestingly, there were few, if any, branded whiskeys or commercial distilleries. Instead, more than 100 barrel blenders purchased whiskey from farmers in the region who distilled their leftover grain to create a cash crop.

Consumers would visit a barrel blender, usually with a clay jug, as glass bottles were not widely available yet. The consumer would get their jug filled with a whiskey blended to their taste preferences. This process was used around the world. In Scotland, grocer John Walker, of Johnnie Walker Scotch fame, was a barrel blender.

In the mid-1800s, all bourbon was customized to the customer's tastes. This discovery sparked a "Eureka!" What if we returned bourbon to its roots, enabling everyone to have their bourbon their way?

We tested the idea on consumers and got record-setting results. We then did a Fail FAST Fail CHEAP experiment of a custom bourbon experience and got equally positive results. This idea led to a couple of years of negotiating with state and federal regulators, inventing new equipment for bottling custom bourbon a bottle at a time, and developing an in-person custom bourbon experience.

The impact on our profitability was immediate. When we sell a bottle of bourbon, state and federal governments receive a little over half the revenue we collect. However, with the custom bourbon experience, we keep nearly all the revenue. When you blend an offering where you keep 50% of revenue with one where you keep 100% of revenue, you have a more viable, profitable business.

The next challenge we faced was how to scale custom bourbon. The idea worked great at our distillery, but that was a local business, not national. After exploring many options, we settled on franchising the custom bourbon business opportunity.

Soon our first WoodCraft Bourbon Blender franchise store was opened in Louisville, Kentucky's Whiskey Row (Main Street). We require franchisees to use their own Brand Name. And thus Barrels & Billets—A WoodCraft Bourbon Blender was born. Today, we are in discussions to open more franchise locations across the USA and eventually the world.

The idea of enabling everyone to have their own bourbon is simple. The hard part was not the idea. The hard part was problem-solving HOW to make Custom Bourbon feasible. Making it "real" involved never-ending problem-solving and collaboration between marketing, operations, finance, regulatory, and supply chain.

Insights for Managers of Proactive Employees

1. COACHING PROBLEM STATEMENTS: First and foremost, coach for clarity. Help your team members write their statements so that it's impossible to misunderstand their WHAT and WHY. After reading their statements out loud, ask them, "Is this precisely the problem?" and "What specifically do you need ideas for?" Be supportive in helping them edit their statements to be more clear. It can also be useful to provide prompts such as the ones above to encourage deeper thinking.

2. QUANTIFY PROBLEMS: When faced with a major problem that will require significant resources, it can be very helpful to quantify the size of the problem. This can be done by calculating the negative impacts on quality, costs, safety, growth, etc. It can also be done by asking people how big the problem is and how frequently it occurs. You can do this through a simple survey. The Innovation Engineering cloud-based portal has an automated Problem Survey tool that allows you to input 2 to 12 problem statements for feedback. It then graphs the size and frequency of the problem and provides automatic statistical testing and analysis to give you deeper insights.

3. CELEBRATE PROACTIVE ENGAGEMENT: The first phase of implementing a PROACTIVE Problem Solving mindset is to create an environment where employees "say something" when they see problems. The second phase is when they volunteer to create and implement solutions. Growing engagement in problem identification and solution finding occurs from a combination of employee training in WHAT (problem), WHY (it matters), and HOW (to solve). The training is activated when you provide coaching and support.

A simple way to make the new PROACTIVE Problem Solving mindset visible is to borrow from the Buckeye helmet stickers that The Ohio State University football players are awarded for exceptional play and wins. I've seen something similar implemented with problem-solving. For example, for each problem identified with WHAT and HOW, employees are given a sticker for their toolboxes, lockers, lunch buckets, or walls above their desk, etc., or a small pin or button for their lab coats or work jackets. Employees can be given one sticker/pin for identifying a problem and two stickers for helping solve the problem.

As a workplace fills with PROACTIVE Problem Solving stickers/pins, more and more momentum to become involved builds. Importantly, this type of program celebrates engagement. It doesn't pick winners or losers (as contests do) or use cash "bribes" to create engagement. Dr. Deming taught the value of engagement, not winning or losing. He explained that contests create a company with one winner and a whole lot of losers. For this reason, the Deming Prize for Quality is awarded to every company that has achieved excellence. Some years there are many, other years fewer. Each company earns recognition by doing great things, not by "beating" other Japanese companies.

4. YOUR MOST POWERFUL TEAM TOOL: Blue Cards are the most effective way to engage and enroll your team in solving a problem. The addition of boundaries—"Strategic Exclusions" and "Tactical Constraints"—helps prevent wasted efforts by the team. They focus the team more tightly on what you really need help on. Done right, Blue Cards are VERY CLEAR and highly MOTIVATIONAL.

5. SPARKING THINKING: One way to spark the start of PROACTIVE Problem-Solving is to directly ask for help. To find ideas for helping accelerate product development and productivity, Sundar Pichai, CEO of Alphabet and Google, created what he called a "Simplicity Sprint." It involved asking three questions to all employees:

- What would help you work with greater clarity and efficiency to serve our users and customers?
- Where should we remove speed bumps to get better results faster?
- How do we eliminate waste and stay entrepreneurial and focused as we grow?

6. SHAKING UP THE "SAME OLD, SAME OLD": At the start, you and your team will naturally focus your problem-solving on addressing visible problems and frustrations, which is valuable as it builds confidence and delivers immediate impact.

However, as the manager, your job is also to focus on improving things that are not visibly broken. You can identify these improvement opportunities by making a list of your key work systems and how long it has been since each was meaningfully improved. Then you can engage your team in finding ideas for improving your oldest systems. As your team members learn, they can proactively improve systems that are not "visibly broken," boosting their confidence and capability even more.

CHAPTER 3

Communicating Solutions and Enrolling Others

THERE ARE FEW THINGS MORE FRUSTRATING than finding a meaningful solution to a problem and having it rejected by others who just "don't get it."

This chapter explores a system for defining your idea in writing so that others can understand it as you do. It's a structured communication system that will increase your odds of gaining support for your idea. This system also helps you think deeper about your idea, even if you don't need to gain the support of others.

The Importance of Writing

When your idea moves from your head to paper (or computer screen), it becomes "real" to you and to others. Writing is the first prototype of your idea. It helps you see benefits and barriers more clearly. It is also very fast and cheap. The only hard costs are pen and paper.

New ideas are rarely embraced immediately because many adults are willing to stay with a flawed work system rather than change to a new way. It's almost like they've become comfortable with their pain. In some ways, they're addicted to feeling and complaining about the pain.

Talking about an idea can be loose and unstructured. It's also common that when we talk about an idea, we adapt and change it, depending on who is listening. As a result, the idea becomes fuzzy across our team or organization.

Written ideas are more reliable. They are focused and precise. When your idea is clear, you can share, discuss, and even debate your idea with greater clarity.

Barriers to Writing

Many adults have a fear of writing. This phobia is often a result of negative feedback received in school. Some, like me, found math easier than writing so they decided to be a "math/science" person, not a "writing" person.

As a "math" person, I chose chemical engineering because it required the least amount of writing classes. After graduation, I took a job in brand management (marketing) at Procter & Gamble. I was hired because of my entrepreneurial innovation skills.

About a month after I started as a brand assistant on Coast bar soap, my boss, Barb Thomas, who had a master of fine arts in writing, called me into her office. On the table in front of her was a memo I'd written. It was covered in red ink.

Barb was very clear: "I want you to stop writing."

I immediately felt great joy, as writing was very difficult for me.

She continued, "I want you to stop trying to be a writer. You are a really bad writer. In fact, you might be the worst that's ever worked for me."

Barb's next words would change the trajectory of my life.

She said, "Your writing is horrible, but your thinking is very strong. What I want you to do is to just think onto the page. Use your clear thinking to tell me what you have found and what you recommend."

It took me some time, but with Barb's coaching I found that simply "putting my thinking onto the page" aligned with how my brain worked. It worked so well that I was among the first to get promoted among the class of brand assistants hired that year. I would go on to spend my life as a writer of tens of thousands of ideas for new innovations and now some eight books.

For those of you who have given up on writing, I encourage you to alter your mindset and just write what you think.

I've also learned that I'm a better editor than writer. So instead of overthinking my ideas, I just write them. Once I have the first draft, I can start editing what I have written until it clearly communicates exactly what I'm thinking.

Don't Give up on Those Who Have Difficulty Reading and Writing

According to the National Center for Educational Statistics, 21% of adults in the Unites States (about 43 million) are illiterate or functionally illiterate. Another study by the US Department of Education found that 54% of US adults 16 to 74 years old have a reading ability below a sixth grade level.

It's important not to give up on those who have challenges with reading and writing. The fact they have challenges doesn't mean that they can't think.

This was made real to me in an inventing session I led with a US manufacturing company. Two frontline workers who attended the session were known for their ingenuity. However, English was a second language for them. They understood and spoke English, but they had a difficult time writing in English. This was a challenge at the Create session because the process involves creating, then writing ideas on a Yellow Card.

Fortunately, I learned about the two young men before we started the session. Feeling empathy for them because of my history with writing, I asked if there was someone who could help them. One lady volunteered that she spoke Spanish and would be happy to help. Throughout the day, they were told to write their ideas in Spanish and/or to speak their ideas to her. She then translated their ideas into English on Yellow Cards.

Following cycles of creation, evaluation, problem-solving, and learning, we had a small set of high-value ideas left. The collective team selected two ideas to focus on the next day. Before we broke for dinner the CEO asked, "Who created these two ideas?" The two young men raised their hands. Each had created one of the best ideas. The room immediately erupted into an energetic round of applause. The lady who had translated their words gave them both a high five.

The lesson is: If you can think, you can create great ideas.

If you are truly uncomfortable with writing, partner with someone for help. If you are a team leader, be aware of people's comfort with writing. Take steps to help them get the ideas from their head onto paper. They might have the big idea you want.

A System for Communicating Proactive Ideas

YELLOW CARDS ARE FOR COMMUNICATING YOUR IDEAS.

BLUE CARDS ARE FOR COMMUNICATING YOUR MISSION.

There are many more complicated names we could have used—ideation output, concept card, tactical action proposal, strategic blueprint, 5 P planning document, etc.

Instead, we named them based on the color of the paper we print them on or put as the background on computer screens.

The color blue evokes trust, integrity, and calm. It sets the direction.

Yellow is the color of optimism, imagination, and possibility. It defines the idea.

In our Innovation Engineering system, there are two types of Yellow Cards for internally and externally focused ideas.

YELLOW CARD for Problem-Solving (primarily internally focused): This version of the Yellow Card is the focus of this book. It provides a simple format for communicating your ideas.

YELLOW CARD for New/Improved Products or Services (primarily externally focused): These cards define ideas for new or improved customer offerings. They define your idea from the perspective of a customer by focusing on Problem, Promise, and Proof. What PROBLEM does the customer face? What are we going to PROMISE them with our new offering? What PROOF can we give them that we will deliver on our PROMISE to solve their PROBLEM? Further details on this type of Yellow Card are found in my book *Driving Eureka!*

Both types of Yellow Cards help others understand your idea, why it's important to take action on it, and the benefits of taking action. When adopted by your team and culture, these two Yellow Cards provide a standardized way to communicate and evaluate ideas.

Problem-Solving Yellow Cards have six elements:

1. **NAME:** Ideally, this name suggests the benefit your idea/project will deliver for the group.

2. **PROBLEM:** As described in chapter 2, summarize WHAT the problem is and, when it's not obvious, WHY it's important to solve it.

3. **SOLUTION:** A simple explanation of your idea in one or two sentences.

4. EXPLAIN HOW IT WORKS: A longer description of how your new idea might work to solve the problem.

5. REINFORCE KEY BENEFITS: The improvements that the idea will generate.

6. SUGGEST EASY NEXT STEP: This is an easy experiment or cycle of learning that can help the organization learn more and build confidence and courage to pursue it.

The structure of a Yellow Card for problem-solving is borrowed from the Persuasive Selling format that I learned at Procter & Gamble. It's the foundation of the famous P&G One Page Memo that is used to turn ideas and insights into action. The purpose of Yellow Cards/Persuasive Selling is to engage others in the potential for ideas.

You start by sharing information on the problem to get the reader interested in learning more. You then explain your solution. Keep it simple and brief. Details come in the next section. Note that this is the reverse of how most people present. Most want to give you the gory details of the idea, the "how" it works, and then finally state the idea. Starting with the idea makes it easier for everyone to follow your thinking.

Having set up the problem and solution, you now explain how it works, providing the details on what will be done differently.

You then explain the three benefits of the change you are proposing. Clearly articulating the benefits helps to create "pull" for your idea from the person you are pitching.

Lastly, you suggest an easy next step. Rather than go for "changing the world" all at once, you suggest a simple action that will help you and the organization learn more.

The simple elements of the Yellow Card make it easy to translate your idea into a practical and "supportable" reality.

Getting right to the idea up front can make you feel uncomfortable at first. It can feel like you are boasting or being dictatorial with your solution. However, when you give your listener a brief outline of your idea in a way to generate interest, you are actually HELPING THE LISTENER understand your idea.

When you go into the many details before saying your idea, the listener is left wondering, "Why should I care about this?" or "Why am I being told this?"

In time you will get comfortable with this approach. In fact, you will be so comfortable that you will find yourself unconsciously flipping into this structure as part of ordinary conversations.

You will summarize your problem to get alignment with others before suggesting your idea. You will do this in your professional and personal life:

Problem—Summarize the situation.

"We've talked about doing something more active for a vacation."

Solution—State your idea.

"What if we did a guided walking tour across Scotland?"

After you explain how it works, you reinforce the key benefits of your idea,

> *It would give us motivation to get in better shape. The cost is actually about the same as we spend for vacation now. And it would be a great adventure for our children to do with us.*

Rather than trying to "close the sale" immediately, you then suggest an easy next step.

> *I've heard that the Websters have done a walking tour of the wine country in California. It's not the same. But what if we asked them over for dinner to share their experience?*

Problem

As detailed in chapter 2, Problem Statements summarize the situation you face. They help the reader understand WHAT the problem is. And, when it's not intuitively obvious, they also articulate WHY it's important that we solve this problem.

The goal is to provide information, insight, and/or data that open your listener to learning more. You summarize the listener's pain or challenge to find common ground as you state with clarity WHAT the problem is and WHY it's important to solve.

Great Problem Statements create interest, curiosity, and a desire to learn more from those you are pitching. They understand and connect with the situation you are describing.

State the Idea

Here you get right into it. You state with clarity what your idea is. You don't want listeners to have to guess where you are going. You want them to know where you are going so that, as you tell them how it works and the key benefits, they have a frame of reference.

Importantly, your idea needs to have a SIMPLE AND OBVIOUS connection to the problem you summarized. For example:

PROBLEM: Our field people spend two hours a day doing data entry, leaving just six hours to do work.

Solution: Create a one-input system. As we place the order, it fills in some of the paperwork, so the field person can simply complete the form.

PROBLEM: Half of our production staff have back problems.

Solution: Add a roller conveyor so we can push production units on the floor instead of lifting them.

PROBLEM: Patients must wait about an hour for lab results. This clogs up our patient rooms and waiting area.

Solution: Install test equipment in our lab for the simple and fast tests. Have a staff person from the lab run tests three mornings a week—when we schedule these patients. This could double our capacity.

Explain How It Works

At this point the person you are pitching is very interested. He or she understands the situation and has a basic understanding of your idea to address it.

With Explain How it Works, you provide details, building confidence that your idea will solve the problem. We have found three communication structures useful for this stage of the process.

1. **DEFINE STEP BY STEP:** Here you define your solution in easy-to-follow steps:

STEP 1: *SORT daily customer orders based on shipping region.*

STEP 2: *PRODUCE all orders and stack on one pallet per region.*

STEP 3: *SHIP the pallet without having to do secondary sorting and stacking.*

2. **DEFINE NOW AND NEW:** This approach draws a direct contrast between the current approach and the new approach.

NOW–*Currently we hold 10 standing meetings each week.*

NEW–*Keep two meetings weekly and move the other eight to every other week in person, with digital updates in between when necessary. This schedule cuts live weekly meetings from 10 to 6.*

3. **NEW TECHNOLOGY:** When a new technology is available that is not commonly known, explain how it can help solve the problem.

> *There is a new technology that our machine supplier has developed that adds a unique "load table" to the front end of our machine. They claim it cuts packing jams and reduces starts and stops of the line by 80%.*

You are telling your listeners a simple story. Done right, you may get a few questions for clarity, but the conversation stays focused on how your idea will help resolve your problem.

Reinforce Key Benefits

At this point, your listeners understand the problem, your idea, and how it works. However, change is hard. It usually takes more than a simple understanding to convince others to support and take action.

We gain their commitment to support our idea by articulating THREE key benefits. And, yes, I capitalized THREE on purpose. I don't know why, but there is great value in the power of three.

Procter & Gamble teaches using three reasons. Three was also the number of points I was coached to state when I cohosted a national radio program distributed by Public Radio International.

Your three reasons can be a mixture of benefits for your external customers (help them reduce costs) as well as for your department or company (help us become preferred supplier). They can be benefits for today (we can save 20% immediately) and for tomorrow (this gets us aligned with the growing trend towards recycling). They can be tactical (it grows our programming capacity) and strategic (it sets us up as a preferred employer with new programmers.)

Benefits help you close the sale. They create "pull" for your idea by answering the question that your listener may have as to "WHY should I care?"

It's important to state benefits, not features. Features are what you are doing or what is being done. Benefits are how what happens delivers value relative to your problem.

An augmented reality visual system that lays words over shelves as you walk the warehouse is a feature. An augmented reality system that helps reduce warehouse "pick times" by 40% is a benefit. A grill that allows you to cook with fire is a feature. A grill that gives you truer outdoor BBQ flavor is a benefit.

If relevant, explain how easily and/or inexpensively the idea can be tested or implemented, especially when the details are not obvious because the idea is unique.

Benefits can also be personal. State how this change will help listeners, who might be wondering if you have an ulterior motive. Honesty about your motivation creates more trust between you and your listeners. The key is to be very honest.

Suggest an Easy Next Step

In the language of "selling," this is where you close the sale. Make it easy for your listener to say yes.

It can be an easy way to get started: "Run a small test of the new approach." It can be learning more: "Ask an expert or get a second opinion."

To make your "next step" really easy, estimate the "cost" in time and money:

"It will only take about an hour to learn it."

"It will only cost about $200 to try it."

If You're Very Confident: "It will cost about one shift of production to learn if we can increase capacity by 50%."

Tips on Writing Yellow Cards

1. Freewriting and Reading Your Yellow Card Out Loud: As stated previously, freewriting your idea in as many words as needed is an easy way to get started. Then you organize your thoughts into the structure of the Yellow Card. At this point, reading your idea out loud will help you identify gaps in your thinking. Best-selling author David McCullough also believed in the power of reading his drafts out loud to his wife or having his wife read to him. He explained, "You can hear things you cannot see, redundancies, awkward expressions."

2. Be Specific With Numbers: The power of numbers when summarizing the situation and stating benefits is immense. There is a big difference between "We are wasting lots of time" and "We are wasting 1 hour a day per employee on this." A study we did of more than 3,000 ideas found that quantifying a benefit increases the odds of success with new ideas by as much as 52%. Numbers give listeners an understanding of the magnitude of the benefit you are proposing. Compare the difference of these two benefit statements:

- "We will save money."
- "We will save 22%."

3. Yellow Cards Are a "System" for Telling the Story of Your idea: Yellow Cards offer a system that brings together the independent parts of your problem/idea/solution. The result is a simple story about what problem you are solving, how you will solve it, how it works, the value of pursuing it, and how to get started on making the change or learning more. One part should naturally flow into the next. Therefore, when you make a major edit to one section of your Yellow Card, it's important to check how that impacts other parts of the card. For example, stating a bigger problem as you summarize the situation might then require a stronger articulation on how it works and the benefits.

Final Thoughts on Writing

As stated earlier, writing, like its cousin math, is a subject that adults can have personal challenges with. Somewhere long ago in their education they adopted a mindset that they "can't write" or "can't do math." These beliefs can be deep-seated.

The reality is that writing and math as we use them in PROACTIVE Problem Solving are first and foremost systems to help you think.

Both writing and math are things that everyone can improve on. I think a favorite author of mine said this best.

> *Writing is something that you can never do as well as it can be done. It is a perpetual challenge, and it is more difficult than anything else that I have ever done—so I do it. And it makes me happy when I do it well.*
>
> —Ernest Hemingway

It's important to note that one of Ernest Hemingway's most important books was *The Old Man and the Sea*. It was only about 128 pages long. And it used simple words and sentences. It was written at the level that a fourth grader (9 to 10 years old) could understand.

Insights for Managers of Proactive Employees

1. CONCENTRATE FIRST ON CLARITY: First and foremost, coach for clarity. Confusion is not a strategy for success. Coach your team members to clearly state in writing the idea in their head. They know more than they think. Help them write in simple words. Write so that a fifth grader can understand their idea. Note, it's not that most can't read at a higher level. Rather, the more complicated the idea, the more mental bandwidth it takes to understand. When you write in simple words, those listening or reading are more likely to understand and support your idea.

2. FOCUS, FOCUS, FOCUS: The easiest way to improve clarity is through focus. Strip away needless information. Instead of three problems, focus on the most important one. Instead of five benefits, focus on the three most important. Instead of three next steps, focus on the most impactful one.

3. DON'T BE QUICK TO JUDGE IDEAS: As a manager, you are very busy. When you find yourself ready to give a quick, reflexive NO, stop for a minute. Ask questions to understand the problem and the solution. It is highly likely that the employee is having a hard time communicating his or her idea. By asking questions and really listening, you will stop yourself from saying NO when you should be saying YES. And you will encourage employees to come to you with more ideas, even when you say NO, because they feel that you really listen to them.

4. LEARN BOTH YELLOW CARDS: As someone who manages Proactive Employees, you must understand the difference between the two types of Yellow Cards. As your team members get more comfortable and confident in their innovation work, they will naturally drift to ideas that are focused on ways to improve your products/services for your organization's customers. While these ideas can be valuable, they may be outside the scope of your team's work. They need to be forwarded to those who lead your new-and-improved product/service pipeline of ideas.

PART TWO

CREATING Solutions

4. **THREE PRINCIPLES THAT WILL 5X YOUR PROBLEM-SOLVING**
    - Mind Dump
5. **USING STIMULUS MINING TO SPARK IDEAS**
    - Patent/Wisdom Mining
    - Market/Insight Mining
    - Future/Unrelated Mining
6. **GAINING A NEW PERSPECTIVE**
    - Musical Chairs
    - Homeward Trail
    - Great Escape

7A. INDUSTRIAL-STRENGTH PROBLEM-SOLVING

- Lawbreaker
- PO

7B. INDUSTRIAL-STRENGTH PROBLEM-SOLVING

- Insight for Managers—IE CREATE Sessions

8. PROBLEM-SOLVING SYSTEM IMPROVEMENTS

CHAPTER 4

Three Principles That Will 5X Your Problem-Solving

THIS CHAPTER TEACHES YOU THE THREE PRINCIPLES that will 5X your ability to create solutions to life's problems. That's not 5% or 10% or even 50%, but 500% more effectively!

The three principles have been validated in academic studies and in thousands of CREATE sessions with real world challenges at small, medium, large, for-profit, nonprofit, government, and academic organizations.

The three principles for creating meaningfully unique solutions to your challenges include: Explore Stimulus, Leverage Diversity, and Drive Out Fear.

Dr. Deming referenced similar concepts with different words. What we call Stimulus, he called Gaining More Knowledge. What we call Diversity, he called Cooperation with Others. And, what we call Drive Out Fear, he called Experimentation.

Modeling of the three principles with the number of great ideas resulted in a simple mathematical model. Most interesting is how

Diversity loads into the equation as an exponential impact, proving that Diversity and Inclusion are not simply the RIGHT THINGS to do, they are also the SMART THINGS to do to grow your capability to problem-solve.

Leverage DIVERSITY

# of Great Ideas = Explore STIMULUS

Drive Out FEAR

The way this principle impacts your ability to problem-solve is simple:

EXPLORE STIMULUS: Ideas are feats of association. To create more and better ideas, you need to tap all the stimulus in your brain and fill your brain with more stimulus. You then connect the stimulus to your challenge, igniting what author Dr. Edward DeBono called Lateral Thinking. Stimulus can take many forms. It can be raw ideas, insights, facts, technologies, or even abstract thoughts. Think of stimuli as filling your brain with insights, sights, sounds, smells, and concepts that you smash together into one or more new solutions.

LEVERAGE DIVERSITY AND INCLUSION: Stimulus becomes amplified exponentially when it's exposed to a diversity of mindsets. Our personal mindsets are built from our experiences, our education, and our interests. Different people view the same stimulus and make different connections. This is why enabling diversity and inclusion is not only the RIGHT THING to do, but also the SMART THING to do to create a culture that thinks smarter, faster, and more creatively. Diversity creates an exponential increase in the effectiveness of brainstorming and problem-solving.

For example, a chemical engineer might look at the dynamics of the problem. An English major might look at how the problem is defined and communicated. A 30-something high school graduate who has worked in production for 10 years might look at the practical job at hand. Each viewpoint provides richness to our exploration of new ideas.

DRIVE OUT FEAR: As fear grows, the number of ideas created goes down. Sadly, most ideas are "killed" before we even give voice to them. Adult brains are wired to stop ideas that, at first glance, could be considered foolish, dumb, impossible, impractical, or crazy. In the early stage of idea generation we must learn to turn off our mental filters and give voice to our wild ideas. These ideas then serve as stimulus for additional ideas.

Our research finds that with Mind Dump and all problem-solving efforts, fear has a negative impact on the quantity and quality of ideas. The antidote to fear during idea creation is to leverage the psychology of relabeling to neutralize your emotional response. When an idea has issues that evoke fear—unknowns, risks, feasibility issues, etc.—relabel the issue as a "Death Threat" and continue creating new ideas and insights.

Relabeling fears as Death Threats and setting them aside when creating ideas allows you to explore new options and ideas. Conversely, when you embrace the fear, you stop your thinking, your momentum, and your motivation to create a solution to your problem.

Ideas with the greatest potential for solving your problem will inevitably have one or more Death Threats. To resolve them, we use Plan-Do-Study-Act (PDSA) cycles. These are quick-and-easy learning experiments. The intense focus on "quick and easy" learning caused students to irreverently rename PDSA as Fail FAST Fail CHEAP cycles of learning. Psychologically, this language is also helpful in reducing fear, as it lowers expectations of perfection on any one cycle. Driving out fear with PDSA is so important that it's the subject of Part Three of this book.

Experience the Power of Stimulus with Mind Dump

Mind Dump is a powerful way to experience the effectiveness of Exploring Stimulus and Leveraging Diversity. It's also my starting place for problem-solving.

In simple terms, it taps into the wisdom, experience, and insights that already exist in your head. Every moment of every day, your brain gathers stimulus through your learnings and experiences. This stimulus, when processed, becomes the raw material that sparks new solutions.

The truth is that you know much more than you give yourself credit for. Inside your brain exists many ideas in both your conscious and subconscious memory banks.

Starting with our existing ideas and insights helps us "make room in our brain" for additional stimulus and new ideas. A fundamental truth of human nature is that, until we've pursued our existing ideas, we will not invest time and energy exploring ideas from outside of ourselves.

The first wave of Mind Dump is scanning for previous ideas that could apply to the current situation. It's about looking for a direct link from the current problem to the solution to a previous problem.

The second wave of Mind Dump is accessing parts and pieces of ideas, insights, and wisdom that might be combined into a new idea. It goes beyond direct links to indirect connections that may or may not have usefulness. These parts and pieces are then played with using free association and forced association.

Free association is about letting your mind leap from thought to thought. For example, say my challenge is creating an idea for a special dinner for Saturday night. I may start with thinking about potential themes, foods, what the guests might like or not, what's fresh at the market this time of year.

As I'm thinking, some things seem to resonate with me more than others. When those hit, I let my mind go on a thinking excursion, allowing one idea to connect to another to another. The process takes all of 1 to 3 minutes. Many of these excursions go nowhere. However, the process is fast with very little time wasted.

My wife and I have "theme dinners" almost every Saturday night. The idea is to create a dinner that is meaningfully unique—that stretches our culinary boundaries.

Recently, when thinking of a theme, the name Italian Gravy stood out to me from a recipe book I'd been reading. It's basically a two-part meal of pasta with red sauce (the gravy), then a variety of meats are served that have been finished in the red sauce. Here's my thinking excursion:

1. **CONNECT**—Italian Gravy reminds me of a recipe by author and TV star Anthony Bourdain that he called "Sunday Gravy."

2. **PROBLEM**—The Bourdain recipe was amazing, but it was really complicated. It was also expensive to find all the various pieces of meat it required.

3. **QUESTION**—I now asked myself, "How else could we make the meat unique other than crazy expensive and weird cuts?"

4. **CONNECT**—I think pork, beef, chicken, fish.
5. **CONNECT**—I think loins, sausages, ground, diced.
6. **CONNECT**—I think fried, smoked, grilled, sous vide.
7. **PROBLEM**—How can I do this without spending hours on prep and cooking? I have a bunch of things to do during the day on Saturday.
8. **CONNECT**—How about using the smoker to cook the meats? I could cook inexpensive cuts slowly to make them tender, then finish the meats and some sausages on the grill. Then I could let them simmer in the sauce for an hour while we have drinks and appetizers.
9. **VOILÀ**—a "Gravy and Smoked BBQ" mash up!

The result is a fun idea that takes Sunday Gravy to a new place.

Notice how I allow myself to find PROBLEMS with my ideas and to even ask QUESTIONS. What I'm doing with my mind is a series of rapid Fail FAST and Fail CHEAP (PDSA) cycles of learning. I'm allowing my logical "left brain" to nudge my creative "right brain." This process brings me closer and closer to a practical yet creative solution to my Saturday night dinner challenge.

I can do this in my mind because I trust both sides of my brain. I know that one side is not going to take over and disrespect the other. My logical brain is not going to wrestle the idea to the simplest, cheapest, and most boring idea. My creative brain is not going to push a crazed and impractical solution. Working together, they create a Meaningfully Unique idea.

Learning How to Leverage Diversity Through Mind Dump

Your personal stimulus and insights will spark ideas. Combining your ideas with those of others will spark even more ideas.

Working with others to create ideas requires you to respect their thoughts and notions. You don't need to agree or even like their ideas, but you must RESPECT them.

The more trust you have in one another, the greater your collective success. When there is mutual respect, you play off each other's ideas without judgment. You work together to solve problems and Death Threats. Together you celebrate leaps of imagination and creativity.

Eureka! Ranch research confirms the exponential power of diversity of thought. Separate research finds that when we collaborate with others, challenges seem less difficult. One study involved people standing at the bottom of a hill. When a group of people were asked to judge how steep the hill was, they found it less steep than when individuals were asked to estimate the steepness of the same hill. Similarly, when we work together, problems seem easier to solve. And Death Threats seem less deadly.

Simple Mind Dump

Mind Dump is a "mental thinking" adventure. To maximize effectiveness, record the flow of ideas and insights on paper or a digital screen. My favorite way is to write my ideas and insights on index cards or to use a two-dimensional display thinking process called Mind Mapping that was invented by creativity expert Tony Buzan. It is a method of creating a visual map of your ideas and insights. You start with a main idea in the center of a piece of paper. Then you free-associate on your challenge, writing your first thoughts outside of the center phrase, connecting them with a line. You continue to free-associate ideas and insights, growing your map.

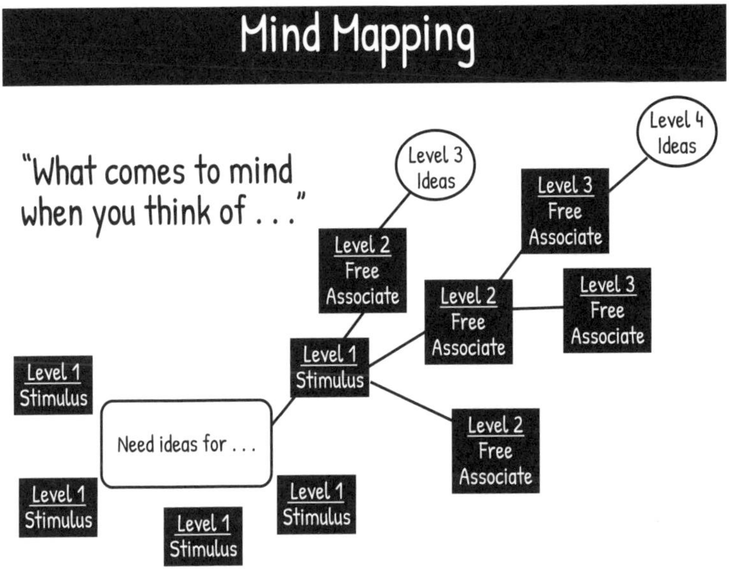

Both index cards and Mind Mapping work. My personal preference is to use index cards as they make it easy to sort and combine ideas. I find that the physical act of sorting cards provides additional stimulus connections for my mind.

Step One of Mind Dump is to write down everything that comes to your mind when thinking about the problem. Write down insights and ideas that you understand, as well as those that, at first blush, you don't understand. When exploring your mind, the following phrases can be useful.

- Think smells, sights, sounds, textures.
- Think the good, the bad, the horrible.
- Think about the ideal answer.
- Think about great experiences/bad experiences.
- Think about compromises and work-arounds that the current challenge creates.
- Think about the simple answer.

Step Two of Mind Dump is to create solutions sparked by the ideas and insights from Step One. This involves connecting two, three, or more ideas/insights to spark solutions.

Idea creation is best done with a playful mind—sorting, re-sorting, connecting, and creating possible solutions. It's a mental exploration of "what if" options. The importance of releasing your mind and trusting your thoughts cannot be overestimated.

> *Before I begin creating ideas I love the feeling of possibility that exists at the start. Mind Dump exercise is a critical way to start the creation of ideas. It captures the pre-existing solutions for the mission. Many times these are the spark that creates a great idea. Other times they set the stage for other ideas that come later.*
>
> —Wendy Ferris, IE Black Belt, InVision Edge

Step Three of Mind Dump is to write your ideas onto Yellow Cards. Writing your idea helps you think deeper. It also makes it easier to evaluate and to share your idea with others.

Step Four of Mind Dump is to evaluate and improve your ideas. Look for Death Threats to the feasibility, effectiveness, and costs versus benefits.

When you first start problem-solving, it's best to make a clear separation between the creation and the evaluation of your ideas. As you become more trusting in your idea creation ability, you will build the capacity to flip from idea creation to evaluation without adverse consequences. The flip makes the creative process go much faster as you make hundreds of iterations in your mind from inspirations to practicality to inspirations for solutions, etc. Be careful when working with others, especially those who are new to problem-solving. Take time to explain the back-and-forth flips from inspiration to practicality in your thinking. Otherwise you will make mental leaps in your thinking that will leave them confused and frustrated.

Leveraging the Exponential Impact of Diversity and Inclusion

Deep inside everyone in your organization is a little voice that gives them ideas. Sadly, many have learned to ignore that voice and kill the ideas before sharing them. In organizations, not speaking ideas often grows into a cultural norm.

Mind Dump is a way for a group to share ideas in a safe and supportive environment. It encourages everyone to share what they know. It tells employees that their ideas and insights matter.

The process with teams is the same as outlined above:

1. *Share your thinking verbally or on index cards or Mind Mapping.*
2. *Create solutions by connecting initial thinking to the problem.*
3. *Write your solutions on Yellow Cards.*
4. *Evaluate and Improve your ideas.*

This process is followed by PDSA cycles to validate and optimize your ideas for a solution.

The importance of every voice mattering was made real many times during a U.S. Department of Commerce project where we provided education and coaching to hundreds of small and midsize manufacturing companies.

The engagements varied in length from hours to days, depending on the situation. They generally involved working with the leadership team of the company. Occasionally a couple of frontline workers would be invited. These were employees who worked in production, programming, frontline sales, delivery, engineering, or even bookkeeping.

In general, they understood technical issues. However, their frontline experience gave them unique insights that the leadership team often didn't have.

Involving frontline staff proved so effective that we made it part of our regular process. Most leaders were very supportive of including line workers. A few were reluctant, citing security and secrecy issues. Others were just against involving them.

One vice president of production stands out for his blunt negativity toward line workers. When I suggested we train and enable workers to create ideas, he said, "Doug, I don't believe it's a good thing to get the workers thinking creatively. They need to just show up on time, do their job, and leave the thinking to us."

I took a big sip of my coffee and paused. His remark was shocking but not surprising. Sadly, the idea of enabling workers is not universally supported yet.

> *My first experience of its power was many years ago, right at the start of my journey into Innovation Engineering. I am British, I am an introvert, and back then I was unsure if I could be "creative." I was in an unfamiliar environment with people I didn't know. In addition, I thought I was about to be called upon to contribute to some kind of brainstorming. Anxiety levels were high!*
>
> *What then happened was simply joyous. We were put at our ease, reminded of the problem we were there to tackle, and given thinking time alone with pen and paper. Mind Dump gives everyone a voice and gently coaxes out all those initial ideas.*
>
> —Helen Potter,
> Innovation Engineering Black Belt, *Eureka! Europe*

Why Mind Dump Works

Mind Dump is based on the simple truth that you know far more than you think you know. Inside your brain is a wealth of perceptions, experiences, insights, feelings, and wisdom.

An article in the May 1, 2010, issue of *Scientific American* estimated that the average human has 2.5 petabytes of memory (or a million gigabytes). This is the equivalent of 3 million hours of TV shows. Mind Dump helps you access more of your wonderfully rich memory.

The structure of Mind Dump helps you articulate and leverage your existing thoughts on paper. Your insights are then fed back into your brain in unexpected combinations, resulting in new ideas for solving your problems.

The simplicity and structured nature of Mind Dump builds your problem-solving confidence by teaching you to trust your thinking.

Barriers to Mind Dump

The greatest barrier to Mind Dump is lack of trust in yourself. From an early age we are told we can't paint, can't draw, can't write, can't invent, etc., and while you may not win a Nobel Prize with your invention, inside you lie ideas that can make a difference in your world.

The secret is to listen. And listening starts with thinking deeply. Mind Dump forces us to become mindful of our situation.

I've found that creativity professionals—be they artists, chefs or scientists—have a high awareness of their thoughts. They also trust that there is a wealth of stimulus that can be tapped into. Without personal judgment, they feel comfortable free-associating between their previous ideas and insights and the challenge before them. They are also very observant of the world around them. They notice original thinking by others, in the marketplace and even in mass media. They then effortlessly free-associate on how their observations can help them solve their current challenges.

Conversely, those who see themselves as not creative stop ideas that pop into their head before they have a chance to become something great.

Confidence in our ability to create ideas is directly related to how safe we feel in our environment, community, or even career.

When an organization or team is in a negative cycle, the creation of ideas is more challenging. Eureka! Ranch tracking studies find that when the economy goes down, many adults become less confident in their ability to create new ideas. I say "many people" because in a major downturn, a few people and organizations hit a point where survival depends on reinvention. It's not uncommon that (especially with a good leader) during bad times they become very open to creating solutions to ensure the survival of their career or organization.

Two Examples of Using Mind Dump

INDUSTRIAL VALVES

I was sitting with the leadership team of a 100-plus-year-old industrial company that made specialty valves for chemical plants. We were talking about their need for new ideas to revitalize sales.

Suddenly, one of the leaders gave voice to the classic belief. "Let's be honest with ourselves. Everything that can be thought of with valves has been done already."

I saw his response not as an "attack" but rather as an admission of his lack of confidence in the company's ability to create ideas.

Without hesitation, I got up and walked to a white board in the room and wrote, "What do we know about valves?"

I then peppered them with questions about their valves, the parts, pieces, and uses. I asked them why they made them the way they did. I asked what they were proud of and what frustrated them about their valves. I wrote all their responses on the center of a white board using their exact words as much as possible.

After about 15 minutes, a wealth of wisdom was written in the center of the two white boards in the room. I then stopped, pointed to the white boards, and asked, "What ideas for valves come to mind based on these insights?"

It started slowly, but soon ideas for manufacturing, marketing, and design were voiced. I wrote them on the board in a ring outside of the first thoughts in a different color ink. Some ideas were met with positive reactions, some negative, and some laughed at. When a negative comment was made, I restated it as, "Yes, that could be a Death Threat." I then wrote Death Threat in the next ring from the center and asked, "How could we solve that?" I wrote the ideas in the next ring from the center. Seeing ideas verbalized, Death Threats identified and Solutions Created changed the mindset in the room. "I Can't"/"We can't" slowly became "Maybe we can!" From this simple afternoon exploration came a pipeline of projects that were implemented over the next year, resulting in record growth in sales and profits for the company.

WoodCraft BOURBON WIZARD

At our Brain Brew distilleries we had many customers who loved the idea of custom bourbon, but they didn't have the time to go through the 1-hour blending experience. This was especially true at Barrels & Billets, our Louisville franchise location on Main Street or "Bourbon Row" because it had lots of walk-in traffic.

The idea was to create an AI-powered WoodCraft Bourbon Wizard that could create custom recipes for distillery guests in 2 minutes.

Fortunately, Eureka! Ranch's team had experience building AI systems that provide expert recommendations.

Mind Dump was the key to creating the Bourbon Wizard. We used it to tap into the wisdom of our three master bourbon makers. Each of us shared our ideas and insights based on our personal experiences. As we shared our thoughts, we discovered new ideas that served as hypotheses that Greg Lemmon, the Eureka! Ranch expert at AI models, tested using statistical modeling of past decisions made by thousands of consumers.

The result was the WoodCraft Bourbon Wizard—MyBourbon Wizard.com. You answer 13 questions on what you like and don't like, and the Wizard creates your custom bourbon recipe complete with tasting notes and customized cocktail recommendations. You can then "taste it by the glass" or "buy a bottle" at our distilleries.

Today, the Bourbon Wizard is very smart. It can often create a better custom bourbon than consumers can create themselves because the AI model has the "thinking" capacity to handle more complexity than most consumers. The model regularly crafts complex and luxurious custom bourbons with four, five, or even six different WoodCraft finished bourbons in which consumers classically blend two or three bourbons.

Pedigree on the Research Behind the Three Principles

Two separate academic studies found that Explore Stimulus, Leverage Diversity, and Drive Out Fear increase the number of actionable ideas for solving business problems by 5X or 500% versus the traditional approach to creating solutions.

The first study was executed and published by Dr. Andy VanGundy of the University of Oklahoma. It involved a series of controlled experiments designed to solve a problem for the Frito-Lay company. It tested the three principles versus a typical free-form brainstorming. Following the experiments, the ideas from each group were sent to Frito-Lay innovation executives to evaluate Meaningful Uniqueness. Dr. VanGundy found a 5X difference in the number of high-quality ideas created when using the three principles.

The second study was a three-year research project involving Eureka! Ranch CREATE Sessions with top corporations from around the world. It was led by Dr. Chris Stormann. The project involved: **(1)** an assessment of the mindset of participants before the session, **(2)** measurements of self-perceived effectiveness every 40 minutes during the creation of ideas, and **(3)** quantification of the number of ideas at the end of the week that the team felt were worth acting on.

Statistical analysis found several significant correlations. There were statically significant relationships between pre-session assessments and overall CREATE session effectiveness and session effectiveness with overall project success at the end of the week.

The research correlations were so strong that we built a CREATE System customization system that we still use today. Before the session, we administer an innovation assessment survey with those who will be participating in the session.

The survey results are used to customize the design of the CREATE session to compensate for team fears and anxieties and to leverage strengths.

Sessions with teams with low innovation confidence and high fear include such things as: **(1)** Specific innovation methods that research finds will be most effective for them, **(2)** A more structured facilitation that "explains" what we are doing to create ideas and why it has been proven to work, and **(3)** Highly empathetic and deliberate one-on-one coaching support.

Teams with high innovation confidence and low fears are challenged to think bigger, bolder, and more adventurously.

Customization of CREATE Sessions based on the mindset of those participating dramatically improved the reliability of CREATE Sessions being highly successful.

The next step in improvement of our CREATE Session system was the development of more effective stimulus as detailed in the next chapter. A few years ago an unpublished tracking study found that, on average, today's CREATE sessions generate a 7X increase in the number of Meaningfully Unique ideas generated.

Insights for Managers of Proactive Employees

1. GIVE PERMISSION TO GO FROM WEIRD TO WONDERFUL: Human nature is for your team members to only tell you smart, practical, and prudent ideas. While this makes them look smart, practical, and prudent, it can also make for ideas that are boring and bland. To open the minds of your team, give them permission to start with the wild. Challenge your team to come up with a half-dozen crazy ideas. Then, as a team, work to transform these wild ideas into wonderfully possible solutions.

2. MODEL A LEARNING MINDSET: Your employees observe your behaviors more than you think. If you are not open to new stimulus and learning, they will be closed to it as well. If you are open to new ideas, speaking phrases such as "I wonder if . . ." "What would happen if . . .?" and "Look at this new thing I just learned . . ." they will be more open to new ideas.

3. ENCOURAGE DIVERSITY: You can leverage diversity by doing such things as: **(1)** Encouraging employees to work together on problems; **(2)** Having each team member talk to three different people about the problem for their insights; and **(3)** Having each team member do a 10-minute search on the internet for different perspectives.

4. DRIVING OUT FEAR: You can help drive out fear by: **(1)** Being an active participant in helping employees solve problems, **(2)** Guiding them to do Fail FAST Fail CHEAP experiments to learn more about their ideas, and **(3)** Working with them to problem-solve their ideas—keeping the spirit of the idea as you make it more actionable.

CHAPTER 5

Using Stimulus Mining to Spark Ideas

STIMULUS MINING ADDS to the rich tapestry of ideas and insights that exist within your brain. It's a journey of exploration fueled by your intrinsic desire to find solutions to the problem you face.

Stimulus Mining Works. It ALWAYS Works.

Stimulus Mining is a disciplined and structured approach to FILLING your brain with fresh stimulus, then using your brain to make CONNECTIONS between your problem, ideas, and the new stimulus. The result is fresh and original ideas for solving your problem. It's as simple as 1 + 1 = WOW!

Poets, painters, and playwrights use the natural world and life encounters to spark new ideas. When poet Robert Frost saw two paths diverge in the wood, he was inspired to write his famous poem "The Road Not Taken."

Stimulus Mining is not plagiarism. It's about using existing ideas and experiences to spark new ways to solve your problem.

Where Mind Dump finds inspiration from inside your memory, Stimulus Mining adds ideas and insights from outside your brain. Then your existing and new insights collide to create new ideas for how to think about and solve your problems.

Stimulus Mining starts with the premise that "You are not special. Someone has probably faced a problem like yours before."

STEP 1—Search to discover an existing solution to your problem from within or outside your industry. The fastest, easiest way to do this is to simply ask those around you for ideas and advice. To maximize value, take notes on what they say. Capture their thoughts as clearly as possible—to increase their usefulness to you when you review them later.

STEP 2—Mine the internet for ideas. Print web pages and take notes when you discover something interesting. The World Wide Web and AI tools make it easy to gather insights and ideas from around the world. In your personal life, you can learn how to change your tire, fix your garbage disposal, or even understand how to bring lithium batteries out of "deep sleep" by watching YouTube videos. But often, the answers aren't as black and white, and there isn't just one way to solve your problem. That's when this technique of gathering stimulus is really useful.

STEP 3—Lay out your learnings on the table in front of you. Then individually or working with others use the stimulus to inspire fresh solutions to your problem.

The Six Most Productive Stimulus Mining Areas

We call the gathering of stimulus to spark ideas Stimulus Mining. The six most productive stimulus mining areas we've identified so far include: Patent, Wisdom, Market, Insight, Future, and Unrelated Mining. Our Innovation Engineering courses offer a deep dive into each of these areas.

The first two Stimulus Mining areas—**Patent** and **Wisdom Mining**—require an investment of your time and energy. They are not easy, as the writing of patent lawyers and academics are both challenging to read (not close to a fifth grade level). However, they are well worth the effort because, like no other stimulus mining, they actually detail HOW to make various "effects" possible. In both cases they are, by design, original work. In the case of patents, they are non-obvious to someone with skill in the art. In the case of Wisdom mining, they make an original contribution to the art.

Patent Mining: Patent applications are "how to" disclosures from inventors. They offer a "cookbook" for solving your problem. Most patents are in the public domain, as they were either rejected or their term of about 20 years has expired. This means the "solutions" described are free for you to use, to improve on, or to combine together with other patents or inventions to create a new patentable innovation. In my opinion, I don't know of a more effective place to find stimulus than by searching patent databases, such as patents.google.com, uspto.org, or a special search engine inside the Innovation Engineering digital tools portal.

Wisdom Mining: University professors and researchers around the world do original research, generating new wisdom. Their research is published in peer-reviewed journals that can be freely used by anyone. As with patents, reading the journals can be challenging, but it is worth the effort. Our Merwyn Rapid Research system at the Eureka!

Ranch was created from insights gained from reading more than 100 academic articles written during the past 60 years. At most libraries you can get an access code to allow you to search databases with full text versions of academic articles for no cost.

The next two Stimulus Mining areas—Market Mining and Insight Mining—are the ones most commonly used by businesspeople to discover new ideas. In the case of problem-solving, they are some of the simplest and fastest areas to gather stimulus on.

Market Mining: In simple terms, this is about looking at how other organizations are approaching the problem you face. This can involve benchmarking versus other companies approaches. The other companies could be in the same industry or a different industry that shares some of the same "unit operations." For example, on a tour of a food manufacturing plant, I leaned how that industry dealt with mixtures of solids and liquids. This observation helped us optimize our WoodCraft finishing system. A fast way to do market mining is to use the internet. One time a team I was working with created a meaningfully unique idea for improving quality from watching a video of the production operations of a company in a different industry. Some of the "unit operations" they use to produce their offering are the same as the company I was working with.

Insight Mining: Classically, this is about asking those who are customers who buy and/or use your product or service. In the case of internally focused problem-solving, you gather insights, ideas, advice, dislikes and likes from those who are directly involved in your problem area and those who are inputs or outputs to your problem area. Simple frustrations they face can inspire new ideas. Things they wish could be done can point to fresh ideas.

The last two Stimulus Mining areas—Future Mining and Unrelated Mining—are by design focused on helping you think proactively and boldly. They are designed to push your thinking to new and original places. They are both very "right brain/imaginative" focused versus Patent/Wisdom Mining that are "left brain logical."

Future Mining: As the name suggests, Future Mining is about thinking about what could be in the future—with new raw materials, new technologies, new ideas. Future mining can be based on trends or simply talking to those knowledgeable about a certain industry on what they see coming in the future. A simple way to do it is called "IF/THEN" as in . . . IF we assume that happened . . . THEN this could create opportunities for. . . . For example, IF we assume that cars will be able to fully drive themselves, THEN a car will be like a bus or train . . . making it more practical for people living farther from cities. The thinking then continues with . . . if we ASSUME this is true . . . then what ideas might this enable.

Unrelated Mining: This mining ignites original thinking. It does this through an adventure of engaging your mind and thinking to a stimulus that has no direct connection to your challenge. For example, you might take a unique painting, piece of music, or even a WOW product or service offering and use it for Unrelated Mining. Operationally, the process involves **(1)** Deconstructing the unrelated stimulus by exploring what comes to mind when you see/think about it, **(2)** Free-associating on your deconstructions to open your mind to fresh thoughts, and **(3)** Exploring connections between your free associations and your problem.

When I'm doing Stimulus Mining, I keep a journal of the ideas I've gathered. I write down everything that seems interesting. It might be a fact, a quote, or a sketch. Some ideas or insights are just raw stimulus—some are beginning ideas.

When faced with a big problem, I often spend a week or two doing stimulus mining. In these cases—every other day or so—usually first thing in the morning, I get a cup of coffee and flip through all the pages I've written. I stop and think for a bit about all that I've read. Then I write a page or two of ideas or observations.

Why Stimulus Mining Works

Stimulus Mining consciously loads your brain with unique insights and ideas. The new stimulus activates your brain to think about your problem from a fresh perspective.

When faced with a problem our natural inclination is to narrow our view to the specific solutions that are immediately apparent. Stimulus Mining encourages us to take a broader view. It applies a "wide-angle lens" to the challenge. It gets us to look beyond our preconceived boundaries as we search for fresh solutions.

Barriers to Stimulus Mining

Ego is the greatest barrier to Stimulus Mining. To make it work, you need to reach outside of your existing perceptions of your problem. You need to be willing to invest your time and energy exploring new ideas even when, at first look, they don't seem relevant. Instead of rejecting the new stimulus as irrelevant, you need to dive into exploring it as a means for igniting fresh thinking.

Opening ourselves to Stimulus Mining requires us to let go of our commonsense judgments. You don't have to let go of practicality forever, but you do need to suspend judgment long enough to allow space for fresh ideas to percolate in your mind.

The practical barrier to Stimulus Mining is the time it can take to gather the stimulus. Importantly, if the WHAT and WHY of the problem engage you, finding the time to gather the stimulus is not difficult.

Four Examples of Stimulus Mining

Wisdom Mining on Illiteracy Sparked Ideas:

The problem we faced involved finding ideas for encouraging bank tellers to sell customers certificates of deposit and other savings offerings. Traditional efforts for encouraging engagement by the bank tellers from training to bonuses to contests had not succeeded. Maggie Nichols (Eureka! Ranch CEO) and I spent a couple days observing and talking to tellers at several branches.

As we were reading through our notes from our Stimulus Mining, it became clear that the tellers were not confident in presenting the savings offerings. They could make the first presentation as they'd been trained. However, they didn't know what to do when customers asked questions. To avoid feeling embarrassed because they couldn't answer questions, they didn't pitch the savings offering to their customers.

To spark ideas, I did Wisdom Mining searches of academic articles on financial confidence. On one of my searches, I typed "illiteracy" and up came an article on compensation strategies used by those who have difficulty reading. As I read the article, I recognized many of the illiteracy compensation strategies used by the bank tellers as well as customers.

I shared the article with Maggie. We developed a hypothesis that a lack of financial knowledge could be a reason why tellers were reluctant to talk to their customers about certificates of deposit.

To confirm our hypothesis, we ran a "financial literacy" test among tellers. The results confirmed that most of the bank tellers were "financially illiterate." As a result, they avoided getting themselves into a conversation with customers that could expose their lack of financial knowledge. They had been taught the "facts" about the bank's offerings, but they didn't have confidence in their understanding of the positives and negatives of certificates of deposit.

To help the tellers, we applied the methods cited in the Wisdom Mining academic article to create ideas for providing more fundamental financial literacy training to build their confidence. We also created presentation materials designed to help the tellers communicate with customers who have a low financial literacy. The result was greater engagement by the bank tellers in pitching savings offerings to customers and customers making a greater return on their savings.

Looking at NEW BOATS Makes me Smart Enough to Buy the Right OLD BOAT: I was looking for a sailboat. I asked friends for advice, and all they did was ask me questions. Questions that, frankly, I couldn't answer.

To find out what I really wanted, I did Market Mining at a major boat show in Maryland. For two days, I got on and off boats. I asked questions of the salespeople, as well as other people who were looking at boats. I saturated my mind with information. In the process, I developed a description of my "ideal boat." It would be wide and stable, and it would easy to set up to go out on the water as well as to close up when returning to the dock. My goal was more time sailing and less "fiddling with stuff."

With my list of requirements I went to three friends who knew boats well. Within minutes of reviewing my requirements each named some boats that might fit my criteria. Interestingly one boat brand—Nonesuch—was on all three lists. I figured if all three suggested the same boat, it was worth a look.

As it turns out, Nonesuch is exactly the boat I described. It was designed by a group of sailors who were tired of working so hard when they went sailing. These boats are very stable and comfortable, and you can be off the dock in 10 minutes and closed when you return just as fast. As one person wrote on the internet, "The best thing about them is you can come about and not put your drink down." A search of the internet found several of them in Saint John, New Brunswick, Canada, not far from my uncle. I called and explained my criteria. He agreed that the Nonesuch was perfect, then checked out the ones that were for sale. Soon I was on my way to Saint John to look at them.

I used Market Mining of new boats to help me learn enough to find my sailboat. It's perfect. And most important of all, my wife of 40+ years also LOVES the boat we call *Winnijean,* named after my great-grandfather's boat.

Unrelated Mining Inspires New Athletic Shoes: A high-performance athletic shoe company came to us looking for new ideas for basketball and running footwear. The winning ideas were inspired from Unrelated Mining. We pulled together a collection of video clips of running—robots, cartoon characters, and wild animals. We watched them at full speed, then at slow motion. Sure enough, while the cartoon characters were by no means "real," the motions imagined by the cartoonists were fascinating. The wild animals' leg movements were also inspiring. With the video as stimulus—we then engaged the team in free-associating fresh ideas. Participants said the first ideas that came to their mind. Others built on those comments. In time, a collection of WOW ideas was created.

The Power of Patent Mining: The number of times over the past 50 years that patents have inspired wicked cool ideas are too many to count. From our system for WoodCraft Finishing of Bourbon—to new potato snacks—to ideas for nonprofits—to ideas for pizza accessories. Patents often teach entirely new ways of solving challenges. In the background discussion section of patents you can get knowledge that will save days or even months of work. Each patent is unique. Reading how a dozen inventors attacked the same problem is mind-opening. Often, new ideas are sparked that combine two, three, or more of the approaches.

Brain Brew offers a demonstration that Patent Mining is not simply theoretical. Early on in the process we ran some experiments with no success. No matter what we did, the bourbon tasted horrible. I pulled all the patents I could find on whiskey aging systems. Eureka! In the patent literature there was a very old patent from the Soviet Union where an inventor proposed a system for accelerating the development of brandy. And, in the U.S.A., I found a couple of patent applications that had been rejected for various reasons by the US Patent Office. I compared and contrasted the various inventors' approaches. The methods were interesting, but all of them seemed unlikely to work as stated. However, reading what they proposed sparked dozens of nonobvious leaps in our thinking.

Final Thoughts on Stimulus Mining

Stimulus Mining is a state of mind. It's about adopting a mindset fueled by a curiosity to learn as much as you can. The best thing about it is that the more you do, the more you have.

Over the years my brain has been filled with minutiae from stimulus mining on thousands of challenges. I am always amazed at how many times I find stimulus I learned 10, 20, or more years ago to be valuable in creating a solution for a problem of today.

Insights for Managers of Proactive Employees

1. COACH EMPLOYEES TO LOOK FOR DISRUPTIVE THOUGHTS, NOT WHOLE IDEAS. It is rare that stimulus mining finds fully formed solutions. Rather, you will find disruptive facts, insights, and technologies that cause you to stop and think. These facts disrupt your comfortable thinking patterns. Mixing together your existing insights with stimulus mining insights can spark fresh ideas.

2. LEVERAGE DIGITAL SEARCH, PHOTOS, AND VIDEO. When I founded Eureka! Ranch, we used Polaroid instant cameras to capture insights. We sent Eureka! Inventing participants out with a Polaroid to mine for insights at places like EPCOT, Universal Studios, and the streets of London. They would come back with photos that were used to spark new ideas. Today, with the power of the internet and mobile phones with amazing cameras and video recorders, the process is even easier. Encourage your team members to take photos of the steps and details involved with their work process. Looking at the photos individually and in sequence can often spark new insights.

3. USE SPARK DECKS TO MULTIPLY THE IMPACT OF STIMULUS MINING: The stimulus mining by you and your team can be presented informally, each person telling what they found, then spending time thinking about how to connect the stimulus with your challenge. A more disciplined way to present stimulus is through the use of Spark Decks. They are simple slides that are Disruptive and Divergent. The left side of the slide contains the Disruptive stimulus learning, insights, facts, photos, video, etc. The right side of the slide contains one to three Divergent prompts to spark ideas . . . what if? . . . how could we? . . . what would happen if . . . ? A classic way to use the Spark Deck slides is to present three to six Spark Deck slides to a team. Then the team splits into groups of two to six. They free-associate on the stimulus—sparking idea starters.

Disruptive Fact
(quick research)

Built-in wear-indicator device with a sensor and microprocessor.

It can measure and report the use history of the shoe and feature.

A display that shows the current point in the shoe's life cycle.

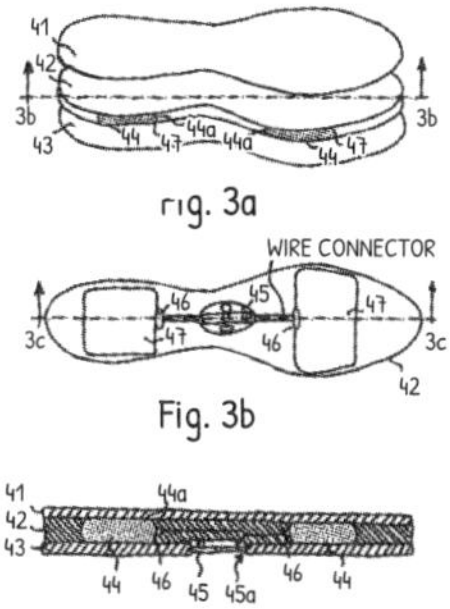

Fig. 3a

Fig. 3b

Fig. 3c

Source: US 6.578.291B2

Divergent Prompt
(idea starter)

- What problem might we solve or prevent with the built-in sensors?
- What information could we promise?
- How could we offer the smartest shoes on Earth?

CHAPTER 6

Gaining a New Perspective

YOU'VE REDUCED THE SIZE AND SCOPE of your problem by using a combination of Mind Dump to think of insights and ideas plus stimulus mining to spark additional ideas.

Despite your progress you feel there must be another way to solve your problem. However, your brain is STUCK. You just see the same ideas over and over again.

This chapter outlines a set of three methods that will help you gain a new perspective and get you "unstuck." The three methods—**Musical Chairs, Homeward Trail,** and **Great Escape**—are designed to open your mind to seeing the problem from a different point of view. They are an "AND" not an "OR" to the methods in the previous chapters.

Musical Chairs helps you look at your problem from the perspective of other people. It literally changes the mental frame of reference you are using to solve your problem.

Homeward Trail takes you back to the origin of the situation around your problem. It helps you understand with greater depth how the problem occurred.

Great Escape taps into your subconscious mind to uncover stimulus and connections that are not obvious to your conscious mind.

Musical Chairs

A Simple Way to Change How You Look at your Challenge

Musical Chairs uses the power of other points of view to solve your challenge.

It's about suspending your preconceived notions and looking at the challenge before you with fresh eyes.

Simple Musical Chairs

The simple way to do Musical Chairs is to just embrace the mindset and thinking of someone else. Think . . .

- What would they do?
- What would they recommend?
- What is most important to them?
- What is least important to them?
- What would bring them the most joy?
- How might they address the problem?

For example, if you are looking for ideas for where to go on a family vacation, explore ideas from the perspective of every family member. Don't quickly dismiss any point of view if it conflicts with your own. Embrace such viewpoints and think as they would think.

In a work setting, you might look for ideas for what your best customers, occasional customers, or former customers might think. Or consider how various other employees or company departments might think about your challenge.

It's important to think deeply about what the other person might think and why. First thoughts can be based on simple stereotypes.

When you go deeper, more profound and impactful ideas are often generated.

Musical Chairs Insights

A way to tap into the impact of Musical Chairs is to LISTEN to what others think about your challenge. The most important question you can ask is "why." Why do you feel that? Why do you do that? Why is that a big problem for you?

For example, Eureka! Ranch was asked to discover ideas for helping community college students who don't have consistent access to food. The project took a leap forward when we spent time face-to-face, listening to students as well as nonprofits focused on helping the students.

As I listened to frontline staff at food pantries, it became clear that addressing their food challenges was about much more than simply food. A complex set of local, state, and federal rules made it challenging to act. In addition, a lack of cooking skills and equipment made the challenge even more complex.

We spent multiple days listening at multiple sites near two rural community colleges. I wrote over 200 ideas or partial ideas, all inspired by the conversations. These ideas became the fuel for a CREATE Session at each school with key stakeholders from the community, school faculty and administration, as well as students. The result was a collection of fresh ideas for addressing food insecurity on campus.

The Fastest and Easiest way to Leverage Musical Chairs Insights

Listening, and listening face-to-face, is invaluable in helping understand the problem from the perspective of others. The downside is it takes time.

Another way to leverage Musical Chairs involves mentally adopting the mindset and even stereotypes of actors, athletes, politicians, historical figures, or even fictional characters from books, plays, TV, or movies.

In my case, I have several personal "heroes" that I often turn to for inspiration. They are people who have taught me a distinct way of thinking. Others are historical figures who I've not met but have read a good amount of their writings.

A full list of the people who I leverage to create ideas would go well into the hundreds. Yes, hundreds. In fact, I've made it something of a hobby to collect the wisdom and mindset of distinctive thinkers.

Here's a short list of some special people whose minds I leverage regularly. In each case I challenge myself to think, "What would they do?"

- What would Ben Franklin (American Founding Father) do?
- What would Dr. W. Edward Deming (Pioneer on System Thinking) do?
- What would Ross Love (VP of Marketing at P&G and mentor) do?
- What would Copthorne MacDonald (expert at wisdom and mentor) do?
- What would Maggie Nichols (Eureka! Ranch CEO and mentor) do?
- What would Joe Girgash (Brain Brew COO and cofounder) do?
- What would Patty Giavara (disciplined engineer and deep thinker) do?
- What would Ken Grier or Eric Schultz (marketing wizards and mentors) do?

I've used these people as inspiration so often they have become my "alter egos." As a result, it takes just seconds for me to look at an issue from the perspective of . . .

- Ben—maintain a sense of humor and mischievousness.
- Dr. Deming—take responsibility for long-term success.
- Maggie—think and link short-term actions with long-term mission.
- Ross—think global not national, regional, or local.

- Joe—confront reality on the operational challenges.
- Patty—think logically and confront reality.
- Ken and Eric—proper and prudent is for losers—break all the rules.

Why Musical Chairs Works

Musical Chairs sparks new ideas by opening our minds to fresh ideas by reducing our personal prejudices. As we live and experience life, we develop prejudices against certain foods, drinks, music, entertainment, and even ways of working.

Personal prejudices are part of what makes each of us an individual. They are not useful, however, when it comes to opening our mind to new perspectives, insights, and ideas.

By shifting your point of view to that of another, you give yourself permission to think differently. When you release your mind, you can see new ideas.

Barriers to Musical Chairs

The greatest barrier to Musical Chairs is not letting go of your personal prejudices. To be effective, you need to remove your personal judgment and adopt someone else's mindset.

Sometimes our prejudices run deep. We may have lived with them since childhood. Giving them up, even for a few minutes of brainstorming, is not always easy.

Focusing on "empathy and understanding" instead of "judgment" is useful. However, even today, after more than 50 years of innovation, I still am amazed at my own "blind spots" when it comes to empathy and understanding. I still find myself in a conversation with someone when I realize I am not fully listening to and understanding what they are saying. Instead, I'm comparing and contrasting their thinking with my preconceived ideas, looking for validation or contradictions. When I notice, I make a conscious effort to listen more intently to what the other person believes and why. We can't change who we are. However, one of the most effective means for bringing new ideas to the world is to listen to other people's ideas.

Three Examples of Musical Chairs

What Would Admiral Peary Do?

For reasons that really don't make logical sense, I made a spontaneous decision to go on a dog-sledding expedition to the North Pole. The adventure would help raise money for a charity I'd founded called Great Aspirations! that helps parents inspire their children.

We would be traveling to the North Pole in the footsteps of Admiral Peary's last dash there. I felt a connection to Peary, as he was born in Fryeburg, Maine, where my grandparents lived. He was also innovative. He invented many of the systems that are used by expeditions today.

Having just read his classic book *The Secrets of North Pole Travel,* I sat down to think, "What would Admiral Peary do to make our expedition more effective?" While it was nearly 100 years later, the issues were the same—care of the dogs, sled design, weight of gear, cooking, clothing, melting ice for water.

After reading the book, it became clear that a key to success in the high Arctic was having an efficient way to melt ice into water. Without water, an expedition would quickly come to an end.

This was so important to Admiral Peary that he spent hours redesigning his expedition's stoves to increase efficiency. The more efficient they were, the less fuel they would be required to carry on their sleds.

Instead of focusing on the stove, as Admiral Peary did, I focused on reinventing the pan used to melt the snow. I pulled together a team that included Jeffery Stamp and the Paderno Pan company.

We did many experiments. We observed what happened as ice and snow melted in a pan. As we watched, an idea was inspired to change the bottom of the pan. Instead of flat, the bottom of the pan would have a giant indentation. Sort of like a bunt cake pan with the center pushed up about a third of the way from the bottom.

The idea was that this could increase the surface area of ice and water with the heat of the bottom of the pan. In addition, having a cone in the center of the pan would concentrate the heat, resulting in faster melting of snow into water and thus using less fuel.

I've inserted a section from my book *North Pole Tenderfoot* for the rest of the story . . .

The only problem with the pan was its weight. It weighed almost twice as much as the regular pot. A few days into the trip leader Paul Shurke was concerned about the pan's weight and if it was worth it.

"Doug, if that pan doesn't do what you say it does out here on the ice, it's going to Davy Jones' Locker—and we've got an easy access point here at our open water camp site."

Gulp. We set both pans on burners, sitting on the ice, We loaded both with snow. And turned the burners on full throttle.

I watched. I waited. Watching a pot boil is especially painful when you're having to think over what you're going to say when you return.

As the first load of snow melted no difference was seen. I was getting worried. I looked for a sign that Paul was kidding. I didn't see any.

The team was feeling a little beaten up. And I was guessing that Paul was going to have the pan "walk the plank" as an example to us all.

I shoveled in another load of snow into each pot. Then another. Watching. Waiting for a sign. The pots were filled about a third of the way with water. Just up over the center cone of the Paderno Polar Pot.

Then a miracle occurred. The snow added to the Paderno pot melted faster. Soon I found myself adding snow twice as often, three times as often to the Paderno pot.

Our new pot didn't melt the first load of snow faster. Probably because the pan was so much heavier any gain in heat transfer was lost as the heat was soaked up by the metal.

However, once the pan got water in it, the center cone acted like a heat amplifier. The snow melted as it floated by the cone. And, the center cone created a natural circular flow—rising in the center and sinking to the outside.

The pan was filled with boiling water in HALF THE TIME!

"It works, it works," I screamed as I did a little dance.

Paul just smiled.

I'd like to think that in heaven, Admiral Peary smiled as well.

Inventing Disney Customer Experiences

Over the years I've had the honor of working with the Walt Disney Company on the creation of new resort experiences. These projects stretch my mind, as they involve problem-solving on how to create a seamless experience from unique resort activities to food and lodging to transportation and facility design.

We often start this type of problem-solving project with a collection of profiles of the target customer for the new resort. We then immerse ourselves in discussions of the customers, their habits, preferences, and mindsets toward vacation experiences. When creating the Disney Institute, we had the team write out "Day in the Life" narratives to define the mindset of guests before, during, and after the experience. This process pushes us to see the resort through the eyes of potential guests.

Thinking as guests would think opens everyone's eyes to insights, ideas, and solutions that are much more exciting and engaging. Interestingly, the biggest ideas for customer experiences often go beyond physical and tangible elements. The things guests remember most are the emotional journeys that they experience—the wows, the surprises, the personal transformations.

$2,000 for a Charge Card?

Back in the late 1990s, an executive from American Express called me with a unique challenge. They were looking to create what they called an American Express Centurion Charge Card. It was to be their most exclusive card. Colored black, the card would be made of anodized titanium. It would cost $2,000 a year (today it's $5,000 a year, plus a $10,000 one-time sign-up fee).

I laughed on the phone. She laughed with me and explained that, yes, she realized that, in a world where credit cards are free, charging $2,000 was challenging. However, there were rumors that American Express had a secret black card. They even get calls asking for it. The company's research found that a high-end American Express card was a potential business opportunity for servicing the super wealthy.

We used a *Lifestyles of the Rich and Famous* Musical Chairs to alter our thinking. With a healthy amount of laughter and jokes, we went beyond material things to psychological and emotional needs and desires.

In the end, the best ideas clustered around three general themes. Each offered something that, even with all the money in the world, it was difficult, if not impossible, to realize.

One of these ideas was to create systems that "anticipated" card holder needs. For example—when a flight got canceled, the Centurion team would immediately start working alternatives before the customer called to ask for help.

Given that AI systems were not yet common, finding a way to execute this benefit was a challenge. We did another Eureka! Session to invent systems for doing many of the initial ideas.

As a member of the initial team, I got one of the first Centurion Cards, along with Jerry Seinfeld, Oprah Winfrey, and Beyoncé. About a year after the card was introduced, the value of "anticipating" customer needs was made real to me at LaGuardia airport. I was on a plane headed to the runway when the pilot pulled the plane out of line and stopped it. About 15 minutes later he announced that, because of a warning light in the cockpit, we were returning to the gate. He also added, "I'm really sorry for this, as this flight will be canceled for tonight." He then added, "Before you go crazy searching, I've been advised there is only one other flight to Cincinnati, and it has only two seats on it."

Instantly, there was a dash to phones to get one of those seats. Before I could dial, my phone rang. It was American Express Centurion. "Mr. Hall, this is American Express Centurion. We saw your flight was canceled. You are booked on the other flight—it leaves in 20 minutes, and the gate is four down from your current one."

Now that was a WOW! Since I was sitting among a group of very grumpy passengers, I kept my joy to myself.

Over time, the core principles articulated during that project have lived on. Another principle for the Centurion Card was to provide card members "special access." This year my wife and I will enjoy two "once in a lifetime" Centurion Living experiences that are curated specially for Centurion Members. In the spring we attended a day-long experience in New York City with cellist Yo-Yo Ma. The event included lunch and three 90-minute sets where he spoke on creativity; did unique duets; and provided deeper-than-normal perspective on the music he was playing, who created it, and who first played it. As intended, it was a very intimate event with about 40 people in attendance.

Just as with Disney, the Centurion project involved using Musical Chairs to think deeply from the perspective of customers.

Homeward Trail

Homeward Trail is a variation of Musical Chairs. It is worthy of articulating as a separate method because of its record of success. I would estimate that this method helped me discover about one-third of the biggest ideas I've ever invented.

Homeward Trail is about going back to the birth of the problem, situation, product, service, company, or even a production system. It's about learning about the origins of the situation—the facts, the surrounding conditions, and motivation for the original solution. It's also about learning about changes that have been made in the system/product/situation over the years—both what improvements were made and why they were done.

When you understand the origin and the evolution of the problem in front of you, then your mind is opened to fresh insights. This is not about "replicating" the past, but rather using it as inspiration for new ideas.

Homeward Trail involves all aspects of the challenge. In the case of products, this means the origins of the product design itself, as well as the origins of the marketing and packaging of it.

Looking into the origins is about respecting the original creators' work. It means understanding the world as they saw it as well as the tradeoffs they were required to make at the time of creation.

Simple Homeward Trail

The most effective approach to Homeward Trail is through first-person exploration of the origins. This means walking the production line, it means meeting with those who were involved in the creation of the challenge. It also often involves the same exploration of significant changes that have occurred since the birth of the original idea.

Success with Homeward Trail requires an open and respectful mindset. It involves learning what they created and why they did it as they did. As you understand the origins, your mind will become saturated with new appreciation for the challenge you are working on solving. As you pull back and contrast the origins with today, new ideas will be sparked. New technologies, new understandings, and even new raw materials will open up new opportunities.

Don't be surprised if you conclude that over the years the original intent of the idea has drifted from its original purpose. And, as a result an idea worth exploring is returning the system, the product, or service to a new version of what it was originally.

It's possible to do Homeward Trail by reading about the birth of the idea or watching video of the founders talking. However, it's far more impactful to do it live and in person. Words and video are representations of a three-dimensional reality that is far more complex and interesting. When it's live in front of you, you see, smell, hear, and feel the energy of how it all comes together. Just as when you are talking to the actual creators you gain deeper insights.

Understanding the whole gives you an appreciation that is far deeper than simply understanding the parts taken separately. In the process, you learn the "system" that makes up your challenge. This allows you to visualize and understand the interconnections that make up your challenge.

Understanding the origins of the creation sparks ideas and lays a foundation for your future idea creation. There are two other approaches to Homeward Trail that are also useful.

Homeward Trail Version 2: Observing Magic Moments and Consequences

Here, the focus of your exploration is on the impact the thing you are creating ideas for (the system, product, service, etc.) has on the world.

Examples include:

- The impact your role in the production line has on departments "down the line."
- The impact your role in the hospital has on departments "down the line."
- How consumers use your product or service.
- How your students use what you taught them.
- How your customers make purchase decisions based on your packaging presentation.

Again, as much as possible, you are doing this in person. You are looking for two things: Magic Moments and Consequences. Magic Moments are effects that delight. Consequences are negative effects. In both cases, the purpose is for you to be able to understand the system that surrounds your problem and its interconnections.

This approach takes time. During the first hour or so of observing, your mind will focus on the obvious. During the second hour, you will start to see things that you missed at first. Examples of when I've done this, and it led to breakthrough ideas, include:

- Watching folks walk past nonprofit booths at a festival and seeing what makes them stop and take deeper notice.
- Watching consumers in a grocery store make purchase decisions for a dairy product.
- Observing a factory packaging line to understand the workflows and the impact that a change in one area of the line has on other parts of the process.
- Watching how students of Innovation Engineering approach "Lab Classes" after watching a set of videos on a specific lesson.

Homeward Trail Version 3: Listening to Those Closest to the Work

My father taught me to listen to those who are closest to the work. He found that machine operators, technicians, and lab assistants have a unique understanding of issues that are not obvious to most executives.

Listening to those who have "been there and done that" can be invaluable. As you listen and learn, stay open to ideas that are different from what you believe. Ask questions to understand the why and how something is done.

Why Homeward Trail Works

Creating anything meaningful takes a lot of time and energy. Those doing the creation are sweating hundreds of little details. They are also making hundreds of tradeoffs and pivots as they go from idea to reality. The thinking that makes up this journey contains lots of wisdom.

Homeward Trail works because of the genuineness of the stimulus. It can be the wisdom of those who created the system, product, service, or whatever you are working on. It can also be the wisdom of those who are "customers" for the output of the challenge. Or it can be the wisdom of those who are closest to the production or operation of the idea.

First-person wisdom has authenticity that resonates at a deeper level than a representation of that wisdom, be it written, audio, or video. It's the same with original paintings versus prints. At the Ranch we have a high-end signed print of Norman Rockwell's *Freedom of Speech* painting. It's a glorious painting that celebrates the freedom to speak your mind and be listened to. The print is amazing; however, the original at the Norman Rockwell Museum in Stockbridge, Massachusetts, is breathtaking. So, too, I've found first-person Homeward Trail learning to be equally breathtaking.

Barriers to Homeward Trail

Homeward Trail requires an investment of time and effort. Again, it requires us to open ourselves up to the ideas of others. As such, big egos are the greatest barrier.

The older I get, the more I realize I have much to learn. Sadly, some adults feel a need to be smarter than everyone else. Instead of celebrating the wisdom of creators or frontline workers, they view them as not very smart. This is not helpful.

What is helpful is to use past failures as a source of learning. Stop, listen, and learn why we pursued the failed idea and what caused it to fail. There is as much to learn from failures as there is from successes.

A simple way to activate a positive mindset toward past decisions is to embrace curiosity. Open yourself to learning the mysteries of why past decisions and actions were taken.

Embracing curiosity is about a desire to learn and to know more about something or someone. When you let go of your preconceived thoughts and open yourself to new insights, you will realize the exponential impact of diversity and inclusion.

Examples of Homeward Trail

When you start looking for Homeward Trail insights, new opportunities will present themselves. Over the years I've found insights from Homeward Trail that sparked fresh ideas. A few examples:

- Walking a factory in Mexico with the plant manager who had been with the plant from when it opened sparked areas to explore for fresh ideas. As we walked, he explained not only what each piece of equipment did but also why it was important in the absolute. This tour gave me a three-dimensional understanding of how the various parts of the factory worked together as a system to create their products. It also identified areas to explore for new ideas.

- Spending an afternoon with retired machine operators and manufacturing engineers talking about the biggest ideas they had for improving operations that the company never pursued.
- Visiting a national history museum with a company founder in a country that was new to me, so to learn about their culture and how the past influences their views of how they look at risk.

Three Deeper Examples

What Did Great-Grandfather Do?

A family-owned furniture company had a problem with scuff marks on their furniture. The cause seemed to be the wood surface. Today's woods and treatment processes resulted in wood surfaces that were too soft.

A great-grandson of the founder remembered hearing stories as a child about an invention that was patented by the company for increasing the strength of wood surfaces. After digging through the corporate archives, he found the patent number. This allowed him to look up the patent on the internet. VOILÀ! A 120-year-old patent filed by his great-grandfather described a process for making the surface harder and less likely to get scuffed!

I LOVE this story. The great-grandson went on to tell me he had been trying to solve this problem for a couple of years. The situation became urgent when competition started using his company's "soft" wood as a reason for retailers to move away from selling the company's products. Amazingly, the answer to their problem had already been found years before.

This experience is an example of why I am fearful that wisdom is being lost in our digital world. I love the convenience of digital files. However, I miss file cabinets with files of original documents. At Procter & Gamble, when I took over a brand group, I would spend a couple of Saturdays reading the file cabinet from the person who had the job before me.

I read the actual documents—**(1)** Five years of budget reviews with their plans and projections, **(2)** Basis for Recommendation documents that documented why new marketing programs, products, or advertising campaigns were being recommended, and **(3)** Market research studies on habits, practices, and attitudes.

Having a full understanding of how the brand had evolved made me a better brand manager. Having a file cabinet of paper copies made it easy to review the important documents. Today, with digital file cabinets, it can be a challenge to find the original documents that laid out the thinking that was present at the start of projects. The result is lost wisdom.

Junk Warehouse Gold

At a manufacturing plant, I explained that I was looking to understand the origins. I wanted to walk the production plant from start to finish. I wanted to know what they did and why. I also wanted to know how they'd changed over the past 70 years since the plant was built. I also wanted to see any old equipment that had been tried, as well as prototypes built for experimentation.

The tour was epic. I scribbled 50 ideas as we walked the plant. But the real gold came when we went to the junk warehouse. In this building were the relics from failed production ideas. They kept them because, as the manager said, "You never know when someone will invent again something we've tried in the past." On about six rows of steel shelving sat equipment, prototypes, molds, and production parts.

I walked the shelves, poking into boxes and lifting parts as I asked for the story of each thing. Amazingly, the managers giving the tour knew the story behind 80% of the stuff. I madly scribbled more ideas.

At the end of the fourth row, on the top shelf, I found gold: a special machine they had tried that failed for cost reasons. When it was invented, this machine was state of the art. Today, in our digital world, it was an antique. However, in that machine was the essence of an idea that, with today's technology, could be transformative. I snapped photos and asked for more details on how it worked and the failure of the machine.

About a month later, the team came to the Eureka! Ranch to invent ideas. Hundreds were invented—maybe a third of them sparked by insights from the Homeward Trail visit to the manufacturing plant. The biggest idea—one that could literally double the company's sales—was sparked by that failed machine. Importantly, the final idea went from the original machine through about eight generations of evolutions to the final idea they are pursuing today.

A Big Dunk in Wisconsin

This is an example of how the Homeward Trail sometimes isn't about going back 70 years—sometimes it's about simply going into the field to see, feel, and experience what employees are working on.

It was the end of October and I was north of Green Bay, Wisconsin. It was cold and cloudy. The purpose of my trip was to get an understanding of the capabilities of a new type of personal watercraft (jet boat) that a major company was developing. They were looking for help developing a persuasive marketing message for it. To keep it secret, they were designing and testing it in this very remote location.

I met with the two designers and they were excited to see me, as no one from the corporate office had ever made the trip. As planned, they put me in a wet suit and a crash helmet. We walked to the lake to experience two expensive prototypes for the new machine. They explained the very unique features they'd built into the prototypes. They then did a demonstration for me as I sat on a competitor's jet boat.

Then it was my turn. I did as they said, doing turns at high speed. Then, as they instructed me, I hit a straightaway and pulled very hard on a special lever that acted as a brake—before I knew what was happening, the nose of the boat dove into the water, then the machine shot into the air like a dolphin. As I went airborne I leaned to the right, the machine twisted, and I went splat into the very cold water. They rushed over to check on me, laughing the entire time. All I could do was laugh as well. It seems they had purposely not told me to be gentle with the brake. It was basically my "baptism" into the team. They then gave me several other demonstration tests to run, to showcase the amazing effects they had designed into the two prototypes.

Later, in a local pub with a cold craft beer and a warm bowl of stew, they told me all the details of where they started—what they learned on their journey creating this machine. They also outlined the next three generations that they saw in the future. As they talked, it became clear that they had built something amazing. It also became clear that the corporate office had not taken the time to fully understand it. The corporate office had read their reports and the results of water tests. However, no one had actually visited and experienced this piece of amazing engineering.

At the CREATE session that followed, I was seen as a genius. I shared my experience. I gave full credit to the engineers. From this we developed a marketing campaign that testing indicated was very persuasive. The project was given the green light to go to the next stage of development. Sadly, about a year later, a corporate reorganization caused the Personal Watercraft project to be shut down. I wonder to this day what happened to the two prototypes up in northern Wisconsin. My guess is the two engineers have them and are having a ton of fun riding them.

Great Escape

Great Escape is my "go to" when I need to think bigger and bolder.

Where Mind Dump captures your conscious memory, Great Escape taps into your subconscious mind, allowing your millions of brain cells to make connections between all that you've learned and experienced.

In simple terms, Great Escape embraces a mindset of letting go and stepping back from the problem in front of you. It does this by giving space to your subconscious brain through a multitude of methods such as visualization, meditation, rhythmic exercise, or even napping.

Great Escape is not "voodoo magic." It is a real method for discovering real ideas. Legendary examples of scientific breakthroughs powered by the subconscious mind include Mendeleev's discovery of the periodic table of elements, Wallace's discovery of natural selection, Kekule's discovery of the structure of benzene, and Descartes' discovery of the scientific method.

At the most extreme level, Great Escape enables you to visualize a new reality with high levels of complexity. In the *Sloan Management Review,* editor-in-chief Michael S. Hopkins' tells of Apple Founder Steve Jobs's ability to "see ideas" during a visit between Jobs and Edwin Land, inventor of Polaroid instant photography.

Michael explained it this way:

> *Dr Land had been kicked out of Polaroid. He had his own lab on the Charles River in Cambridge. It was a fascinating afternoon because we were sitting in this big conference room with an empty table. Dr Land and Steve were both looking at the center of the table the whole time they were talking. Dr Land was saying: "I could see what the Polaroid camera should be. It was just as real to me as if it was sitting in front of me before I had ever built one." And Steve said: "Yeah, that's exactly the way*

I saw the Macintosh." He said if I asked someone who had only used a personal calculator what a Macintosh should be like they couldn't have told me. There was no way to do consumer research on it, so I had to go and create it and then show it to people and say now what do you think?

Both had this ability to not invent products but discover products. Both said these products have always existed—it's just that no one has ever seen them before. We were the ones who discovered them. The Polaroid camera always existed, and the Macintosh always existed —it's a matter of discovery.

Simple Great Escape

I find Great Escape is most effective after I've filled my brain to the brim with insights and ideas. The process enables me to make new connections between the information I've packed into my cranium and the problem I am attempting to solve.

Great Escape gives space to subconscious connections by quieting your conscious mind. There are many ways to do this. The four that I use most frequently include:

1. Visualization: After intensely thinking about the problem, I stop, close my eyes, and slow down my mind. Sometimes I slow my mind by counting 20 breaths. Other times I visualize myself in a relaxing situation. For me, I find it effective to think of myself sitting beside a lake or the ocean—feeling the wind and sounds of the water. I then let my mind go blank. When non-relevant thoughts enter my mind, I mentally recognize them and let them flow through me. Eventually deeper, bigger thoughts and connections start to reveal themselves. When a particularly surprising idea comes, I stop and immediately write down the idea and everything else that is attached to it. I don't stop to talk. Or get up from where I am sitting. I then usually close my eyes and continue the process till I have a half dozen or so ideas.

2. Freewriting: As described earlier, this is a particular favorite of Innovation Engineering students. It is a classic tool of writers. It involves taking paper and pen or a keyboard and writing nonstop for 3 to 5 minutes. I start with "I need ideas for . . ." then just write. As I write, new ideas are sparked that I follow with more writing. When my thoughts slow, I ask myself one of the five W's of journalism—WHO, WHAT, WHEN, WHERE, WHY. For discipline, I often set a timer to force myself to keep writing and not stop. I've found that when I feel I have nothing more to write—if I keep going—some of the best ideas reveal themselves.

3. Aerobic Exercise: When I'm particularly stressed and frustrated, I will often get up, get out, and do aerobic exercise. When writing books during the winter at our Canadian farmhouse, I go cross-country skiing across the farmland. When creating ideas to solve a problem at our distillery, I will go for a walk around the lake at the back of our property. If it's summer, I go kayaking or biking. If the weather is bad, I might get on a treadmill or exercise bike. There is something about the repetitive action of aerobics, at a moderate intensity, that can help reduce mental chatter and in the process enable connections to the subconscious mind. I have found that high-intensity exercise, while good for the body, tends to use up my mental capacity, blocking all ideas. Just as with freewriting, I prefer activities that force me to go for a specific amount of time, like jogging or kayaking the perimeter of the lake or the farmland.

4. Guided Meditation: I believe in Great Escape. So much so that I've created a number of guided audio meditations specifically for problem-solving. My favorite is called "The Island of Innocence, Truth and Wisdom." It was created over 20 years ago, and it remains amazingly effective. It's a 12-minute audio that takes you on a journey where you mentally "tell the story of your adventure" three times to three specific people: **(1)** to a child (innocence), **(2)** to one of your most trusted friends (truth), and **(3)** to a mentor (wisdom). Each time you tell your story, they ask you questions that force you to think deeper. As the audio comes to an end, you are instructed that upon the sound of three bells you are to open your eyes and do freewriting of "that which you understand and that which you don't." But don't take my word for it—try listening to the Great Escape recordings by visiting PROACTIVEProblemSolving.com.

Why Great Escape Works

The ability of our brains to capture and remember stimulus is immense. As I wrote in the Mind Dump chapter, the average human has 2.5 petabytes of memory (or a million gigabytes). This is the equivalent of 3 million hours of TV shows.

Much of what we know is not readily accessible to our conscious mind. The National Institute of Health found that our conscious brain is in charge of our thinking about 5% of the time, and our subconscious 95% of the time.

However, much of this knowledge is in deep memory. Great Escape works by relaxing the conscious mind and allowing the deep memory of the subconscious mind to make connections and be heard.

Great Escape also stops us from overthinking our problem-solving. Many adults carry into their idea creation lots of "stuff" such as their prejudices, their fears, their anxieties. All of this uses up mental energy, reducing their capacity to make idea-generating connections.

Barriers to Great Escape

Great Escape requires you to trust your subconscious mind. If you are new to idea creation, this can require a leap of faith. This is especially true if you've been working really hard to create ideas for some time. The idea of just relaxing and not "thinking hard" can be especially hard to trust when you are under pressure to find a solution to your problem. Those who have a mindset that is more "left brain logical" can find trusting their subconscious to be especially difficult.

Another barrier to Great Escape is communication of the ideas you discover. With Great Escape, you are looking at the same problem but from a different perspective. Your brain is making conscious and subconscious connections. These connections are being processed, tested, and revised by your brain in nanoseconds. Research indicates that our conscious brain can process about 50 bits of information per second, whereas our subconscious and visual processing capacity can process 10 million bits per second.

The result is that when your thinking process comes to a stopping point and you speak your idea—others may look at you bewildered. They have not been on the same mental journey.

In these situations you need to find the patience to explain your idea and how you got to it.

Why I Personally Love Great Escape

I love the FREEDOM that Great Escape gives me to think. When creating ideas, the brain is filled with conflicting needs and demands. This disrupts your thoughts. Great Escape frees me from this "noise" and allows me to focus my undivided attention on creating ideas that address the challenge before me.

I also love how it helps me explore DISRUPTIVE IDEAS. With Great Escape, I can set aside negative thoughts and let my mind go on flights of imagination.

Lastly, I find it the fastest way to get UNSTUCK. It is the fastest way to get over the inevitable "speed bumps" of problems that occur. Great Escape is how I wrote the first draft of this entire book in 29 days. Every day I wrote. When a block occurred, I used Great Escape. Every day I used one or more of: visualization, freewriting, and aerobic exercise to work through blocks to my writing. Bottom line—Great Escape WORKS!

Great Escape Ideas

VISUALIZATION OF A COMPUTER MODEL: The challenge was the creation of an AI model for predicting the success of new products and services. We'd spent months running statistical analysis of the data and feeding the data into computer models. No matter what we did, the model just wasn't good enough to be useful.

One evening, I took home a pile of printouts and did a long reading of them. Then I closed my eyes and took a mental trip to the shore of New London Bay at our Canadian farmhouse. As I relaxed . . . my mind journeyed through the data. Suddenly I found myself inside a three-dimensional matrix of data. I was fascinated by the view but did not at first see the value of it. Then, seemingly out of nowhere, I saw a set of patterns. While we had been modeling primarily in two dimensions or in exotic multidimensional models, the actual data aligned cleanly in three dimensions.

I opened my eyes and wrote down my thoughts. The next morning we built a three-dimensional model in about an hour that was more effective than months of work. Eureka! (Sorry, I couldn't stop myself from writing that). That model, named Merwyn in honor of my father (it was his first name), has gone on to be amazingly effective. It's been validated by dozens of multinational companies, in the marketplace, and even by one of the US government's top NIST statisticians (NIST is National Institute of Standards and Technology).

CREATING A SYSTEM FOR FESTIVAL EVENTS: Shortly after our Brain Brew Distillery opened for consumer sales, we were invited to have a booth at a bourbon festival event. The event would feature numerous better-known distilleries. Our challenge was how to stand out from the crowd.

I did the Great Escape Guided Meditation. In the meditation I told the story of our adventure three times—to the innocent child, the trusted friend, and the wise one. As I was mentally telling my challenge to the child, I described the crowd, the booth, and that we would be serving the four bourbons that make up our Riverboat Collection—Show Boat, Paddle Wheel, Deck Hand, and Tall Stacks. As the meditation continued, I mentally told the story again but this time to a trusted friend. As I told the story of my problem,

I suddenly realized that—with four products—it would be difficult for consumers to carry four samples. I also realized that all the other distilleries would have the same problem.

After I did the meditation, I sat and wrote my observations and insights. I also started free-associating on ways to make it easy for bourbon lovers to try all four of our products. From this, an idea was born for a flight tray. Basically, it's a disposable tray that looks something like an artist's paint palette with four holes in it that fit the small cups we serve our samples in. The tasting cups sit down into the holes, making it easier to carry and taste from without the spilling that can happen with classic beer flight trays.

I quickly found some cardboard and cut out a prototype to validate that it would be easy to carry the flight of four bourbons in one hand and sample with the other. We had some printed up with the names of the four samples near the holes for the event.

The flight trays were a huge hit. I'll never forget walking down the aisle to our booth and seeing person after person walking with a flight tray of our bourbons or the four cocktails we made from them. As you'd expect, seeing the flight trays got visitors asking our customers where they got them. Our booth quickly attracted more customers than the other eight distilleries near us combined. All because of a simple tray that allowed consumers to easily stand and sample four bourbons.

Final Thoughts on Gaining a New Perspective

Gaining a New Perspective methods are not additive, not multiplicative. They offer an exponential ability to help you discover and develop more Meaningfully Unique solutions.

They are about embracing how other people think. These include people you agree with and, just as importantly, those you disagree with. They are about honoring every person's perspective without prejudice or prejudgment.

They are about giving up our personal prejudices by applying the mindset of others. By being open to how others look at the world, we experience an exponential increase in our ability to create fresh ideas that can solve our problems.

The reality is that some 85% of the population lives in a left brain, logical world. It's not that they can't go on right brain, imaginative excursions. It's just that they don't have enough experience with it to trust it. With practice, everyone can embrace both sides of their amazing brain.

As I stated earlier, curiosity is the secret. And with curiosity you are guaranteed to become very smart as well as successful at creating ideas. As Ben Franklin wrote,

> *We are all born without knowledge, but curious. With curiosity we should be able to learn as much as possible. With curiosity, it has to take a lot of work to remain ignorant.*

Insights for Managers of Proactive Employees

1. EDUCATE AND FILL BRAINS WITH LEARNING: The foundation of disruptive thinking is to have more "raw material" in your brain. It takes conscious effort for you and your team to become continuous learners. Methods for doing this include: **(1)** Modeling a learning mindset yourself—share your learnings, experiences with team members formally and informally, **(2)** Organize field trips with your team to benchmark, share and learn from other industries and departments within your organization, and **(3)** Put together formal "learning sessions" once a month where you share Spark Decks of future trends and methods and then share insights and ideas.

2. BE INTENTIONAL IN CREATING A CULTURE OF THINKING DIFFERENTLY: It's a fundamental truth that work classically increases to fill the time available for it. If you're not careful, there is no time to think outside of your daily work. To develop a PROACTIVE Problem Solving culture, it's important to be intentional in your efforts. It starts with one-on-one and small-group interactions using what leadership expert Tom Peters called "management by wandering around." The idea is to create moments of unstructured and low-stress interactions. The relaxed mindset of these interactions allows for informal "what if" conversations. More structured approaches include: **(1)** Challenging your team to create "10 wild ideas" for improvement, **(2)** Asking "If you could wave a magic wand, what would you create to make your life better?", and **(3)** Sharing stories of transformation that you've experienced or learned.

3. OVERTLY ASK FOR HELP WITH A YELLOW OR BLUE CARD: Surveys of employees regularly indicate that "not knowing what ideas are needed" is the No. 1 reason why employees don't suggest ideas. Academic research finds a similar dynamic. When teams are asked for "wild," "practical," or any other type of ideas, they create as asked. Overtly asking for help with specific types of ideas is one of the most effective ways to productively create a PROACTIVE Problem Solving culture. You can do this informally or by sharing a Death Threat to a Yellow Card idea you need help solving. Or through a broader request for help through a Blue Card that provides deeper understanding and boundaries. After working a dozen or so problems, your team's creative confidence will grow. Soon they will bring up problems to solve.

4. CREATE A CHANGE AGENT CULTURE: Research by the Eureka! Ranch team for the U.S. Department of Commerce found that to change a culture it was useful to encourage and enable "change agents." These are the people who pioneer a culture of PROACTIVE Problem Solving. They are the "energy source" for changing how a culture thinks and works together. The research found that these types of people exhibited three traits:

a. Entrepreneurial. They were adventurous and aggressive learners who were comfortable with multitasking and uncertainty.

b. Optimistic. Positive attitude, high energy, and a healthy self-confidence.

c. Curious. A personal passion for mining for stimulus, discovering and applying technology, facts, and data.

As a manager, your job is to model and support these traits by encouraging learning, optimism, and curiosity.

CHAPTER 7A

Industrial-Strength Problem-Solving

TRANSFORMATIONAL IDEAS INVOLVE A LEAP OF FAITH. They require you to shake loose from your "adultness" to let your mind run free and unconstrained.

They are an excursion into a new way of thinking about your challenge. Have no fear, the excursion is just a temporary release from your logical brain. You can always return from your leap into new ideas to your existing way of thinking.

With practice, you can shift back and forth from disciplined thinking to dreaming of new ways to address your problems.

This chapter details two of the most reliable methods I know for disrupting your thinking. The first, **Lawbreaker,** is the most direct way I know to discover WOW Ideas. The second, **PO,** is the fastest way I know to open your mind (and the minds of others) to thinking differently.

Lawbreaker

Lawbreaker involves attacking your challenge from the opposite of how you would normally think about it. It does this by overtly breaking the traditions, rules, policies, procedures, and beliefs that are the accepted ways of thinking/working.

There are traditions within every work process, system, and activity in both your personal life and professional life. Most of these traditions were valuable when first developed. However, some of these methods have become fixed while the world around us—technologies, training, experiences—has changed.

At their worst, these once-helpful systems have evolved into rigid bureaucratic barriers to change. The result is that they now generate more pain and waste than they enable.

On the Deming Video series, Professor Russell Ackoff speaks about the importance of redesigning and reinventing systems or products through a mindset he calls Idealized Redesign.

> *The only way that we can think creatively about a system is to assume it was destroyed last night. It no longer exists. For example, the education system of the USA was destroyed last night. Now, if you could do whatever you wanted to right now, what would you do if you were completely unconstrained? If you don't know what you would do when you could do whatever you want right now, how can you possibly know what to do when you can't do whatever you want?*
>
> *This forces you to study the whole instead of the parts taken separately. With Idealized Design you design the system as a whole and then derive the properties of the parts from the properties of the whole. As opposed to analytical design where you start by taking the properties of the parts to drive the properties of the whole.*

We spend an awful lot of time trying to improve things that should be destroyed. We haven't rethought the design of systems for many years. And as they become dysfunctional we institutionalize that dysfunctionality. We have to redesign most of our systems/products and not just improve the existing one.

I recognize that the idea of "blowing up" how you do your fall yard cleanup, your work process, or even the annual big fundraiser for your nonprofit can feel terrifying. Your logical mind tells you, "It's not really broken enough to go through the pain of change."

I can't decide for you what is really bad versus not bad enough to change. What I can say is that it's at least worth doing a "thinking excursion" on what a reinvented system could offer. Just because you think about it doesn't mean you have to pursue it.

Simple Lawbreaker

Lawbreaker begins by making lists of actions that you ALWAYS DO and NEVER DO when working on your problem area.

For example, say your challenge is to find a way to make your morning team meetings at work more productive. Your list of things you ALWAYS DO might include:

- We ALWAYS take 30 minutes each day for our meetings.
- We ALWAYS hold meetings first thing in the morning.

Next, take each of these and challenge them. Adopt a perspective that a requirement of your new idea is to now NEVER DO each of the things you listed as ALWAYS DO.

WE Now NEVER take 30 minutes . . . this could spark an idea like what if we were to split into two meetings a WEEKLY meeting for an hour—focused on bigger issues—and a 15-minute meeting each day on the urgent issues.

We now NEVER hold them first thing in the morning. This could spark the idea of having the meeting at the end of the day—when issues are fresh in everyone's head. It also allows for "incubation" of ideas and thoughts overnight so everyone can start fresh.

The flip side of ALWAYS DO is NEVER DO. Here we reverse the Lawbreaker. We make a list of things we NEVER Do with our team meeting.

- We NEVER allow one person to "take over" the meeting.
- We NEVER make the meetings optional—everyone must attend.

Next, take each of these statements and challenge them. Adopt a point of view that your new idea for your team meetings is to ALWAYS do the thing that you listed.

We now ALWAYS allow one person to "take over" the meeting. This could spark the idea of having a different team member run the meeting each day. As part of this role, they are responsible for providing a 10-minute update on what they are working on personally and what they could use ideas and advice on.

We now ALWAYS make the meetings optional—no one must attend. This could lead to the idea of having each person record a three-minute audio or video update at the end of each day on learnings, issues, and help that they need. Have each audio/video update posted to a digital platform so all can listen and post comments on.

While not all the ideas will work out, the return on your investment of time is fantastic. The process just takes just a few minutes, and just one idea could improve your team meeting every day of every week for a year.

Why Lawbreaker Works

The name "Lawbreaker" engages a mindset of something that is different from the "proper" or "familiar" or "approved" approach to your challenge. The name itself gives you permission to change. Academic research confirms the power of being given direction to your thinking. When teams are given overt permission/direction to "think big" or "think bold" or "think radical," they do so. Wendy Ferris, IE Black Belt at InVision Edge in Winnipeg, Manitoba, Canada, described the Lawbreaker approach this way.

> *We are creatures of habit, and often we get caught up in the complacency of being comfortable or blinded by routine. This is why I really like using Lawbreaker. It drives "what if" scenarios and forces the mind towards change. For example, what if we didn't have access to email to communicate . . . what would we do instead? Lawbreaker is really effective at pushing our thinking forward.*

At its essence, Lawbreaker is about continuing forward with your thinking even when you believe the idea is impossible. Over my many years of problem-solving I've found that perceptions calling an idea impossible are rarely true. You just need to invest time doing some thinking and trust that even bad ideas are useful stimuli for creating great ideas.

The key to success with Lawbreaker is a willingness to let your mind leap to a new place. As your family, friends, or work team build trust in thinking creatively, you can simply say—let's try Lawbreaker. And the collective power of the group becomes focused on bigger and bolder leaps of thought.

Barriers to Lawbreaker

The biggest barrier to Lawbreaker is fear of big changes. Instead of being bold and brave, we seek the smallest, least disruptive way to make incremental improvements in how we work. In work situations, it's common to have spoken or unspoken boundaries on how big of a change your team or organization is willing to accept. This boundary becomes a blockage to our thinking. With Lawbreaker, the goal is to think big and bold.

Because he speaks so eloquently about transformation, I'm going to repeat a section of the Dr. Ackoff quote from the beginning of this chapter.

> *We spend an awful lot of time trying to improve things that should be destroyed. We haven't rethought the design of systems for many years. And as they become dysfunctional we institutionalize that dysfunctionality. We have to redesign most of our systems/products and not just improve the existing one.*

Lawbreaker is NOT One and Done

The reality is that big and bold ideas almost always have negative consequences to other parts of the "system" that surround your problem area. In fact, if your "big" idea doesn't create other challenges or Death Threats, then it's unlikely to be a truly transformational idea.

You need to accept that your big idea will require you to create solutions to the potential negative consequences that your big idea causes to other parts of the "system" you are working on.

At the risk of overusing a case study, our simple idea to enable everyone to have their own Custom Bourbon set off dozens of Death Threats, as it disrupted everything from production to marketing to operations to regulatory issues. Because Custom Bourbon had never been done at scale, Lawbreaker thinking was the only way to find solutions to the multiple Death Threat problems. Here are a few of the biggest Death Threats and how we addressed them.

DEATH THREAT: *Federal and State laws won't allow for custom bourbon.*

It took about a year of problem-solving at both the state and federal levels to register our custom bourbon labels. Our initial applications were rejected as non-compliant. To gain approval, we did a deep dive into the actual rules and regulations of the TTB (Alcohol Tobacco and Tax Bureau of the U.S. Treasury Department). Reading the regulations closely, we found a pathway for making our labels legal. Initially, the revised applications were also rejected, only this time based on other rules we were inadvertently breaking. Nine or so months later, after many cycles of experimentation, we got approval of our formula, label, and products, allowing us to sell custom bourbon legally.

DEATH THREAT: *Consumers won't be able to tell the difference between the bourbons they are tasting.*

Our distillery is grounded in our WoodCraft Finishing methodology. It's based on the simple truth that 70% of the flavor and 100% of the smoothness of Bourbon Whiskey comes from the wood. We started with a set of 24 whiskeys. This proved to be overwhelming for customers. Multiple rounds of consumer testing led us to six distinctly different bourbons, each with a distinctly different taste. The unique tastes are a result of being finished with a unique wood that had been cleaned and toasted to enhance differences: 200-year Oak, European Oak, American Oak, Maple Wood, Cherry Wood, and Smoked Oak.

DEATH THREAT: *Blending whiskey is a difficult skill to learn—consumers will not be able to create a great bourbon to their tastes.*

Borrowing from work we did years ago creating board games and user experiences for the Walt Disney Company, we crafted a "goof proof" journey for our guests. It's a step-by-step system that starts with tasting and leads to a structured process for blending that makes it easy for consumers to craft a great bourbon that matches their taste preferences. The method we use is basically a consumer-friendly version of the actual method that Bob Dalgarno, whiskey maker of the Macallan for 30 years, taught me. It's how he brings together barrels of whiskey from different rick houses to create a luxury whiskey.

One adaptation to Bob's approach that we had to make was to find something to replace graduated cylinders. While Bob can quickly use graduated cylinders for measuring, it takes consumers some time to use them. This is especially true when we explain the need to measure to the bottom of the meniscus or the curved surface of the liquid. With the help of a small business in Vermont, we created and produced a patent-pending bourbon-blending ladle. It makes it easy for consumers to quickly measure and blend their bourbon with higher accuracy.

DEATH THREAT: *It will cost too much to make one custom label and bottle at a time.*

Filling custom bottles manually would make the bottles cost twice the $45 retail price that our research showed was the sweet spot for pricing. To drive down cost, we had to rethink the consumer purchase and bottle production system. We started by creating a digital system that allows consumers to enter the name for their bourbon and their recipe via their phone. Then custom software translates their recipe into a custom label that prints automatically.

To speed the process of filling bottles, the custom label includes a QR code on the back label that contains the recipe for the bottle. The operator simply scans the QR code, then places the bottle in the custom WoodCraft Bourbon Blending machine that we invented and built. In about 30 seconds the machine fills the customer's bottle with the custom bourbon.

DEATH THREAT: *Custom bourbon won't be scalable.*

We quickly found that the demand for YOUR Bourbon YOUR Way was immense. However, state laws make it impossible to ship bourbon to most states.

To grow our business we needed a new route to market. After exploring multiple options, we settled on franchising Custom Bourbon. It took a little over a year to navigate the laws and regulations of franchising. Recently, we opened our first WoodCraft Bourbon Blender franchise on Main Street in Louisville, Kentucky. As of this writing, we've now signed a second, and we expect to soon have many more.

Throughout the Custom Bourbon journey, every time we ran into a challenge we simply put our heads together and figured out a solution. Early on, we had T-shirts printed with a variation of the famous quote from an Apple Commercial, "Some call us the crazy ones . . . and we're OK with that."

You, too, can make the impossible possible. You simply have to love it. You have to love your idea so much you are willing to put in the time and energy required to problem-solve your way to making it a reality.

PO

PO opens your mind to unexpected ideas. It was created by Dr. Edward DeBono. It's a thinking approach that encourages you to confront and reconsider many of the assumptions that you have about your problem. It forces you to consider what might happen if you eliminate something you take for granted, or you reverse or rearrange the order you do things, or exaggerate an element of the problem or simply step back and think of an ideal approach.

With PO we spark the brain to think differently. As Dr. DeBono said during an interview on a radio show I hosted: "The idea is to break the rigid thinking problem. You can't dig a hole in a different place by digging the same hole deeper."

Simple PO

PO disrupts familiar problem/solution patterns with a "PO," which is short for Provocation. The PO statement is designed to provoke your mind to think differently about your challenge.

PO can be done individually, but it is most often done with two or more people.

The process starts with someone making a PO statement. The statement always starts with "PO" to signal to others that you are evoking lateral thinking. The word PO is followed by a seemingly contradictory statement.

For example: If you were creating ideas for a new way to handle overflowing trash cans in your office, you might use an ELIMINATE PO.

"PO There are no trash cans."

At this point, you and those gathered with you simply move your thinking to a place where there are no trash cans. You ACCEPT that suddenly there are no trash cans, and you think WHY MIGHT THIS BE? You don't debate if there should be no trash cans. You accept it fully. You simply MOVE YOUR THINKING TO THIS PLACE. You give voice to why it might be that there are no trash cans.

Your thinking might go like this . . .

- We've gone 100% reuse . . . zero waste or recycling . . . thus . . .
- We've made it easy to wash and store cups for coffee/tea.
- We've moved all printers; we use touch screens to read documents.

- We've limited vending machines that dispense prepackaged stuff.—We've eliminated all but ONE trash can on each floor for the few times it's needed. We've sorted out our vendors who provide food for meetings to do so without waste.

PO statements are obvious contradictions. They are disruptions to proper and prudent thinking. By provoking the brain with a PO that is outside of reasonable, you have no choice but to "think outside the box," which can help you find fresh ideas and solutions. In our example above, thinking of explanations for why there are no trash cans led to ideas for how to solve the problem of overflowing trash cans.

There are no "rules" on what kinds of PO you state. It just needs to be disruptive and unreasonable. DeBono coaches that not all POs will work. Statements can be so disruptive and unconnected that nothing comes to mind. And that's OK. Simply have someone say another. Dr. DeBono suggests five areas as idea starters for PO provocations.

ELIMINATE: Eliminate something you take for granted. Think about the consequences and possibilities for improvement as a result of eliminating a key part, piece, or process.

REVERSAL: Look at the normal direction that something is done and reverse the process. Now think if the process was reversed by placing task B before task A. What impact might that have on the problem?

REARRANGE: Change the normal relationship between parts and pieces of your problem. Now consider the impact, if instead of doing a task for speed you changed the task such that it was used as a means for increasing quality. What impact would that have on your problem?

EXAGGERATION: Take a component of your problem and exaggerate it far outside of reasonable. For example, what would happen if you spent much more time and/or money on the raw materials you use in your production process?

WISHFUL THINKING: This is a leap to the fanciful. It's about letting go and thinking what might the process be like 20, 50, or 100 years from now. Or, what would happen if you could do whatever you wanted to do to improve the process?

One thing I really like about PO is that it's very easy to implement. There is very little preparation or planning involved. It can be activated spontaneously when you need fresh thinking. The ideas are always original—most are not practical—but all are useful leaping-off points for other ideas. It's useful to record all the ideas on paper, white board, or screen for secondary processing into next-generation ideas. This can be done immediately after creating or, even better, do it after a pause of a few hours to refresh your mind.

Why PO Works

Just as with Lawbreaker, PO is about continuing forward with your thinking, even though you believe what you are considering is impossible.

PO is to creativity as Newton's laws of physics are to the movement of objects. It is built on the simple principle of breaking up traditional thinking patterns. This activation of creativity is why, when you are new to a job, you make connections that are new—as you've not become consumed by the established way of thinking. It's also why children can be seen as highly creative: They are not constrained with classic problem/solution thinking patterns.

Barriers to PO

The biggest barrier to PO is the need to embrace an adventurous mindset of curiosity and playfulness. If your self-image is built around a career of being prudent and practical, then PO can create great anxiety.

In the movie *Indiana Jones and the Last Crusade,* the character Indiana Jones (Harrison Ford) comes to a cavern that he needs to cross to save his dad. He stops and checks his notebook for hints on how to get to the other side. As he closes the book, the music swells and he says, "It's impossible. No one can jump this. It's a Leap of Faith." His dad (Sean Connery) who is near death gasps, "You must believe, boy, you must believe." With that, Indiana Jones lifts his foot and steps into the void—only to have an invisible bridge suddenly appear. You can view the clip by searching Indiana Jones Leap of Faith on the internet.

The Leap of Faith that Indiana Jones makes is what is needed to make PO, Lawbreaker, and other disruptive thinking mindsets work.

An Example of PO

100% of Students Achieve An A Grade. The education team at the Eureka! Ranch, along with our partners at the University of Maine, gathered to reinvent how we taught our Innovation Engineering courses in creativity, problem-solving, and innovation. The content was solid. It was grounded in real-world application and quantitative data. What we needed was a new way of teaching it.

The classic approach to teaching college courses—lectures, homework, quizzes, and exams—seemed contradictory to teaching and developing creative skills. The process of exams and tests contradicted what Dr. Deming taught. Exams were the equivalent of "quality inspections" in manufacturing. The more effective approach was to build a system that could drive learning without the need to inspect it.

As we were discussing how we might change our method of education, someone interrupted the conversation with an EXAGGERATION PO: "PO 100% of Students Achieve an A Grade." There was laughter at the thought. We then MOVED OUR THINKING to this place: Think why and how this might be possible.

The conversation that followed led to the creation of a new system of teaching we branded as "Cycles to Mastery." It's a system that enables all who are willing to achieve an A grade. Importantly, they receive the A because they have mastered the content, not because we have made the course easy.

There are lots of elements to Cycles to Mastery. At its core it replicates the iterative learning cycles of the creative process. When students submit their assignments, they are given either a check indicating correct or an X indicating that it needs to be reworked, along with coaching advice. Students have the option of submitting unlimited redos till they have learned and demonstrated their understanding of the assignment.

The system eliminates all tests and exams. In their place is a focus on ensuring that each student has learned and demonstrated mastery of all the course curriculum. This transforms the learning experience. As we tell students, some sections of the course you will get quickly, while others will take more cycles of submission. The good news is if you are willing, we can guarantee that when you invest the time and energy resubmitting, you will achieve full mastery of the content of this course.

Cycles to Mastery has proven to be very effective with 70% achieving a grade of A (2X versus control). Sadly, 30% of students are willing to accept less than an A. This is our next challenge.

Recently, we were excited to learn that the Cycles to Mastery teaching methodology is so meaningfully unique that it's been granted a U.S. patent. This is a significant achievement, as it is very difficult to get a patent on a method of teaching.

Final Observation on Disruptive Thinking: Lawbreaker and PO

Both Lawbreaker and PO are about opening yourself to a new reality. It's like making science fiction real through a series of problem-solving discoveries.

What I like best about both methods is how they spark smiles and laughter from exploring unexpected thoughts and, from the sheer lunacy of many of the Lawbreaker and PO provocations. Laughter is a key reason why these methods are so effective. Research confirms that when people are laughing, they are more likely to open themselves up to nonobvious ideas and insights.

CHAPTER 7B

Industrial-Strength Problem-Solving

Insight for Managers—IE Create Sessions

Innovation Engineering CREATE sessions are covered in-depth in our IE Course for managers of proactive employees as a means to leverage the thinking of a team. That said, anyone can use this system to engage others, be they fellow workers, family, or friends, to find a solution to a challenge.

IE CREATE sessions leverage the exponential power that comes from embracing the diversity of thinking of others. In simple terms, they are a more effective and efficient form of brainstorming. Research by creativity expert Dr. VanGundy, professor at the University of Oklahoma, found that the IE CREATE approach resulted in over 500% more "big ideas" than classic brainstorming.

> *IE CREATE has more stimulus, more focus on the people and the interaction of the people. I'd hate to go back to a regular*

> *brainstorming session after experiencing CREATE. I don't know anybody that does the stuff IE does.*
>
> —Dr. Arthur VanGundy,
> International Creativity Expert, University of Oklahoma

After being taught the PROACTIVE Problem Solving mindset and methods, employees will naturally engage in informal CREATE sessions. Managers should encourage the sessions and, when possible, participate in them. As their confidence in the new mindset grows, managers can and should start to hold formal CREATE sessions. Such sessions are particularly useful when ideas and alignment are needed across your entire team and/or a collection of people from connected departments or business units. They are also a useful way to build confidence across your team in your collective ability to problem-solve.

Why CREATE Sessions Work

CREATE sessions work because of the exponential impact of Diversity.

CREATE sessions provide a system for increasing the quantity and quality of ideas created when a group of people are brought together to problem-solve.

The foundation of the CREATE approach is the work of Alex Osborn, the researcher who invented and gave a name to "Brainstorming" in 1953. Osborn identified two rules for successful Brainstorming:

1. **Defer Judgment:** "Create ideas AND judge" is replaced with "Create, Create, Create, Create, Create"—"build on and refine ideas" and then judge. Instead of killing wild and foolish ideas, they are used as stimuli to spark more ideas.

2. **Quantity Creates Quality:** Groups are challenged to create many solutions for addressing the problem. Having multiple solutions enables further

discovery and optimization, as the solutions themselves can be assembled and reassembled into fresh and productive solutions.

Three things amplify the success of IE CREATE sessions.

1. Clarity of Mission and Boundaries: Classic Brainstorming often interprets Osborn as: All ideas are good. There are no bad ideas. This is a broad interpretation of "Defer Judgment." In most situations, creating solutions without clarity of focus wastes energy. Formal CREATE sessions are guided by a Blue Card that gives participants: **(1)** Background on why it's important to find a solution, **(2)** The focus for the ideas we want, and **(3)** Tactical and strategic boundaries (ideas we are not looking for . . .). Informal CREATE sessions are guided by a simple statement that "Summarizes the Situation." It outlines what ideas we are looking for and why it's important.

2. Stimulus—and Diversity—Driven Idea Generation: CREATE sessions are powered by stimulus and diversity. The stimulus can be shared informally by the project leader, or it can be shared more formally using the Spark Deck system for sharing stimuli. The most effective mechanism for activating stimuli is diversity and inclusion. Each person participating in the CREATE session brings a different point of view, cultural background, and experiences to the session. As such, each person perceives and reacts to stimulus differently—inspiring an exponential increase in the number of ideas created.

3. Yellow Card Structure to Build on and Refine Ideas: For PROACTIVE Problem-Solving, Yellow Cards provide a structure for building on and refining ideas. The process of translating a raw idea into a Yellow Card takes the idea to a second generation of thinking. When writing a Yellow Card, participants often embellish and optimize the original idea based on the multitude of other ideas they have heard during the session.

Simple CREATE Sessions

Most commonly, CREATE sessions are led by managers to enhance the problem-solving ability of a collection of employees. Key steps in the preparation process for a session include:

STEP 1: **Set CREATE Session Objective:** This means a well-thought-out Blue Card. It should give the background narrative (WHY), the mission (WHAT you need ideas for), and Boundaries (strategic and tactical).

STEP 2: **Gather Stimuli:** Ideally, this is done with the help of those who will be participating in the CREATE session. At a team meeting this could involve having them do an internet search using their phones. It could involve them each talking to three other people inside or outside your organization for perspective.

STEP 3: **Translate Stimuli into Spark Deck Slides:** The leader of the CREATE session sorts through all the stimulus mining to create a set of slides that are Disruptive and Divergent. The slides can be words and images, audio, video, or even a hands-on demonstration.

STEP 4: **Create a Playlist for the Session:** CREATE sessions start with personal introductions, then a review of the Blue Card. It then moves to Mind Dump to give space to existing ideas that participants have. Following the sharing of Mind Dump insights and ideas, participants are given a chance to write Yellow Cards. This is followed by cycles of Spark Decks and or other methods as defined in this book, followed by the writing of Yellow Cards.

If you are looking for other methods that have been validated as effective, I suggest my previous books *Jump Start Your Brain* and *Jump Start Your Business Brain.*

Barriers to CREATE Sessions

The greatest barrier to CREATE sessions is that they require time to come together as a group to find solutions. Formal sessions also require preparation: Writing a Blue Card, Stimulus Mining, Spark Deck Creation—to be the most successful.

Psychological barriers to CREATE sessions are resistance to Osborn's rules of engagement: 1) Suspend Judgment and 2) Quantity Creates Quality. Both rules require participants to "let go" of their logical and rational minds. For many, this is equivalent to giving up on the primary mechanism that has shaped their careers: their ability to be focused, not waste time on "crazy ideas," and to be "practical, prudent, and reliable."

To be clear, I am NOT saying that being focused, efficient, practical, prudent, and reliable are not important. What I AM SAYING is that there is a time and a place for everything.

Examples of CREATE Session Ideas

Formal CREATE Session Creates Solution to Production of Custom Orders

The CREATE session featured managers from each of the departments responsible for developing and manufacturing custom orders for the company's food service customers. Large customers would often have very specific requirements for portion sizes, flavors, ingredients, and even packaging.

The problem was that the journey from customer purchase order to shipped product involved many different departments. Each department needed to receive and publish information on each product. The existing system was flawed. As many as 8 out of 10 products had flaws in their data package. The problems were only found at the end of the process, when a team of experts inspected the packaging, product information, regulatory filings, and other elements before releasing the product.

In most cases the flaws were simple mistakes in the documents that accompanied the release of products. However, some mistakes were so significant that they required reworking or scrapping of the product. Even worse, the company had suffered some recalls because mistakes were not caught by the inspectors.

It was an ugly situation. Over the years, as people tried to fix this system, they added more forms, more complexity, and bureaucracy.

At this CREATE session, we divided the production process into four phases. Everyone created ideas for improving each of the phases. Teams optimized and improved the best ideas from each phase with a focus on the overall mission of creating a system that was so "goof proof" it wouldn't require inspection at the end.

The complexity of the problem required two-and-a-half days of work by the team. In the end, for the first time in years, there was a system that everyone believed would make a meaningful difference. You could feel great excitement in the room.

I cautioned that it would take time to build out the programming and to debug the new system. One participant who was part of the inspecting team was fine with it taking time. She explained, "I don't care how long it takes to get it right. All I need is the hope that I won't spend the rest of my life using our current stupid system."

Informal CREATE Session Invents Patented Production Process

With our bourbon business, an informal CREATE session in the driveway delivered a patented breakthrough for us.

Early on we were experimenting with different ways of creating a smoked whiskey. Some of the most prestigious whiskeys from Scotland are smoked with peat. In our case we were looking for an American style of smoked whiskey, a flavor more barbecue smoke than peat smoke. Our approach was to smoke some wood pieces, then Wood-Craft finish a whiskey using the smoked oak pieces. Experiment after experiment was tried and failed. The taste was just not right—it was too light or it was nasty.

One day while watching the smoking go on, we held an informal CREATE session as we watched the smoker in the driveway. Together we came up with crazy ideas—filter the good from the bad smoke, create a wind tunnel to channel the smoke, levitate the wood chips above the smoke, like a skydiver floating in a cloud.

Some ideas made us laugh, a positive indication that we were embracing "defer judgment and quantity creates quality."

As stimulus, I reached into the cloud of smoke floating by and said, "What we really need is a way to get this smoke (grabbing smoke in the air) and not this smoke (pointing to another cloud of smoke)." Again, we all laughed at the craziness of it.

Then someone gave voice to what would eventually be the solution, "What if we distilled the smoke. To keep the good and toss the bad."

When you distill whiskey, you heat the liquid until it vaporizes. As it runs up through the still, you bleed off what are called the "heads and the tails"—taking a middle cut that holds the best taste.

We modified our smoker system to replicate a distillation column. Then, just as when distilling whiskey, we tossed out the heads and tails and took a middle cut of smoke to apply to the wood. It worked amazingly well.

We are very proud of our smoked bourbon. It earned us one of our first double gold medals. And our smoked bourbon was selected by the Arby's restaurant chain to create a bourbon for a national promotion using the same woods they use to smoke the meat for their brisket sandwiches. Incredibly, the product sold out in 1 minute and 52 seconds!

Most exciting, the idea for "distilling smoke" identified during that informal CREATE session in the driveway resulted in an invention that we have been granted a patent on in the US and in many countries around the world.

CHAPTER 8

Problem-Solving SYSTEM Improvements

DR. DEMING TAUGHT that every employee has an intrinsic desire to do meaningful work and that meaningful work provides employees with intrinsic gratification and reward that no amount of extrinsic recognition or reward can match.

He also taught that the primary barrier to doing meaningful work is a broken or flawed "system." He defined a "system" as "two or more independent components that work together to accomplish the aim of the system."

The components of a "system" were defined broadly. They include hard components such as the tools, raw materials provided, standardized work methods, and so on. They also include "soft" components such as maintenance, employee training, staffing levels, communications systems, cultural mindset, and so on.

The importance of problem-solving is made clear with Dr. Deming's teaching that "94% of failures are due to the system. 6% are due to the worker." For example:

- Not being provided proper training is a fault of the system.
- Not being provided the computer power and software needed to work fast is a fault of the system.
- Not having clear standard operating procedures is a fault of the system.
- Not having reliable communications between teams is a fault of the system.
- Not having a culture that encourages and actively supports PROACTIVE organizational engagement is a fault of the system.
- Not having a culture that encourages and supports never-ending improvement is a fault of the system.

A culture that enables PROACTIVE Problem Solving encourages all employees to become an active part of continuously improving the organization's systems and the components that enable those systems.

When employees are unleashed to be PROACTIVE Problem Solvers, their first area of focus is often on improving how they do their work. In time, PROACTIVE employees realize the interconnected nature of their work. They then initiate collaborations with others inside and outside of their work area to make meaningful improvements to the organization's work systems.

Informal and Formal System Improvements

Formal system development or major redevelopment projects leverage the full system improvement process that Dr. Deming taught:

STEP 1: Appreciation for a System. Make the system visible.

STEP 2: Knowledge about Variation. Separate special from common cause errors and variations.

STEP 3: Psychology. Identify and address positive versus negative psychological forces on the system.

STEP 4: Theory of Knowledge. Plan-Do-Study-Act cycles of system improvement.

Our certification courses for Managing PROACTIVE Employees and Innovation Engineering Black Belt explore the four steps in-depth. They also provide training in and access to industrial-strength tools for implementing all four steps of the Deming system.

This book and the PROACTIVE Problem Solving companion course teach an informal approach to problem-solving system improvements. It does a deeper dive into the first two of Deming's steps because these provide the fastest, easiest way to realize success with system improvement. The final two are covered in less depth.

Appreciation for a System

System improvements begin with a conscious awareness and belief in the idea that work is a result of the interconnection of two or more system components. This awareness involves recognizing the presence of systems even when they are not overtly visible.

Systems are easy to see and understand in the case of a manufacturing facility. It's easy to visualize raw materials, pieces of equipment, production levels, and the number of defective products produced.

Systems are harder to see across the modern world of human work systems. Human work systems involve a network of interactions and hand-offs of information, data, and content designed to create a desired outcome. A challenge with human work systems is they are rarely documented and most often exist as a collection of informal procedures between employees and departments. The lack of documentation results in high variation on procedures and work systems.

A particular challenge today is the high number of blended systems that integrate human work, machine work, and or digital/internet systems. These blended systems require an especially disciplined approach to find effective solutions.

Problem-solving of system improvements requires understanding and appreciation of a few simple truths:

- Systems (formal or informal) ALWAYS exist. Employees do not do their work randomly. The human mind is wired to create order out of randomness. When workers start on a job, they seek reliable methods for doing their work.
- If employee work is not defined with formal or informal Standard Operating Procedures, then they will create their own way of doing the work. The methods they create help them get their job done. Once they've found a method that works well enough, they often continue to use it, even if it is not as appropriate, effective, or efficient as it could be.
- For example, a highly experienced worker at a manufacturing company was hired to teach rookies how to work smarter. Shortly after he started, there was a change of management. The new boss told the employee to "just do your work and stop creating new methods and training others." The experienced worker kept creating, but instead of doing it for the good of the company, he did it, as he said, "so me and the boys don't have to work so hard."
- Systems Rarely Change Themselves: If the system gets the job done, most people will keep using it no matter how slow or ineffective it is. A conversation with those who work in a system that is basically "broken" is the essence of crazy.

Q: "Why do you do it that way?"

A: *"Because that's how we do it."*

Q: "Is it a good system?"

A: *"No, it causes lots of rework."*

Q: "Why don't you change it?"

A: *"Not my job."*

SYSTEM RESULTS ARE AMPLIFIED BY THE NUMBER OF INTERACTIONS. Mapping of a system that involved five departments, each with variation in quality, found that, when multiplied together, the potential for failure rose from 5% to 85% if all departments were on the low end of quality on the same project.

A FAST AND EASY WAY TO MAKE YOUR SPECIFIC SYSTEM VISIBLE: There are a multitude of ways to map systems. It's easy to create complex maps that show hundreds of interactions between your system and others across the organization. When starting with PROACTIVE Problem Solving, my suggestion is to start very simple. Start by creating a flow chart that details the sources of variation, inputs, and outputs surrounding your problem area.

A. The process begins with a labeled box in the center of the paper that is the key moment, step, or component of your system you are problem-solving.

B. From the left of the center box, list components that impact your area.

C. To the right of the center box, list component outputs that are a result of the center box.

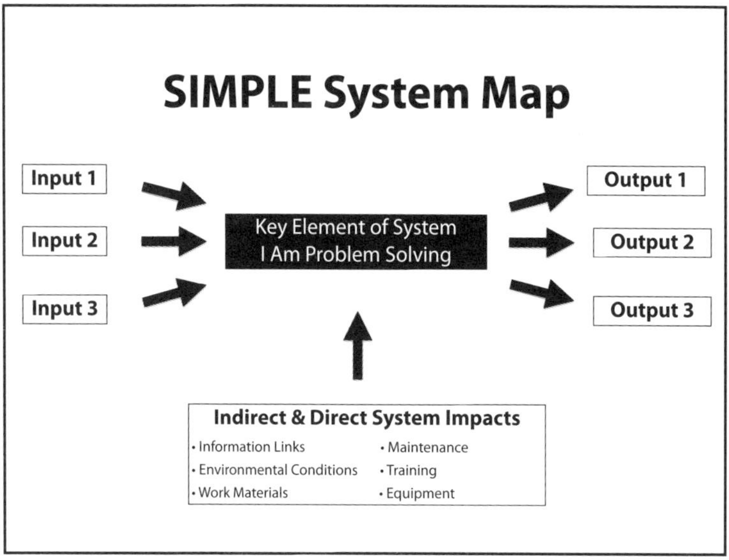

D. Above and below the center box, list other components that impact the work of the center box. These often include indirect information links, as well as the soft systems of methods, maintenance, equipment, materials, environmental conditions, training, and so on.

This creates a very fast and simple visualization of the forces that might be factors in the problem you face.

THE IMPORTANCE OF DIGGING DEEP TO UNDERSTAND ROOT CAUSES. When a problem is identified, the old-world management response is to blame the worker for screwing up. For example, a manufacturing process involved some very expensive parts that had to be handled with special care. Recently, a collection of workers have been identified as creating higher-than-normal damage to the expensive parts. Instead of blaming the workers, the PROACTIVE Manager digs deeper for root causes. This is especially important in this situation because the manager is observing multiple people failing regularly, not just one random event.

A classic technique to get to root causes is called "The Five Whys." It involves asking WHY repeatedly until you can't go deeper and have reached the true root cause of the problem.

Using our factory example, FIVE WHYS might go like this . . .

Q: WHY did the manufacturing employees damage the expensive parts?

A: *The employees hadn't been trained properly on how to handle the parts.*

Q: WHY weren't employees trained properly?

A: *We use informal training—worker to worker—so it's not consistent.*

Q: WHY do we do informal training?

A: *It's very expensive to develop proper training.*

Q: WHY is it very expensive to develop?

A: *We don't have written SOP on what is the right way of doing the work.*

Q: WHY don't we have written documentation?

A: *Because, before this conversation, it was not thought to be valuable.*

Knowledge About Variation

The second Deming principle deals with variation in the components that make up your system. It starts with an understanding and belief that Everything in Life has Variation. Yes, everything. All training, people, equipment, formulations, processes, and products have variation. Variation that doesn't have an impact on the success of the system is acceptable. However, when variation impacts system success, it often sets off a chain reaction of work-arounds that succeed and fail to varying degrees.

Importantly, even our systems of measurement have variation. A company found that the scales they provided to check product weight were causing quality problems. The scales were effective years ago but were no longer appropriate, as the variation across the system had been tightened. They replaced the scales with ones with less variation that read to more decimal points and—voilà—problem solved.

More examples of classic Variation include:

- Variation in training for employees, some trained formally, some informally.
- Variation in raw materials, which includes variation in briefings provided to programmers or ingredients for food production.
- Variation in work systems. Each employee is using a different method because there is no documented Standard Operating Procedure.
- Variation in equipment, as when poor maintenance makes machines vary in output.

Faced with variation that is out of their control, workers must adapt and adjust with continuous work-arounds to produce high-quality work output. This continuous adaptation is mentally and physically exhausting.

Common versus Special Cause Variation

Dr. Deming identified two kinds of variation that can impact a system: Common Cause Variation and Special Cause Variation.

Common Cause variations are built into the system itself. They are reliable variations that happen regularly. Examples include variation in raw materials, equipment, training, or changes in environmental conditions, such as not controlling temperature or humidity in a manufacturing plant.

Special Cause variations are caused by a mistake or random breakdown. Sometimes they are caused by the worker not following the specified work system. This type of error is generally a random and rare event. Examples include the worker who was distracted or rushed and skipped a step, a 100-year flood occurred, or, as we all learned recently, a global pandemic disrupted supply chains.

In the case of a catering company example . . .

Common Cause Catering Problems Include:

- Catering pans that don't stay warm.
- Food recipes that need to be eaten when cooked as they don't "hold" well.

Special Cause Catering Problems Include:

- Forgetting to put out napkins or forgetting to put out napkins before placing silverware.
- Server adding extra salt, making food too salty

When a problem is due to Common Causes, the focus needs to be on fixing the system rather than doing a "search for the guilty."

When a problem is due to Special Causes, we need to confront the source but not overreact to it. This occurs when we add needless rules, inspections, and check offs to make sure it doesn't happen again. These added structures ultimately contribute to the development of a hopeless bureaucracy.

Identifying Common Cause versus Special Cause problems involves three steps:

1. UNDERSTANDING the difference between Common and Special Cause. Knowing the difference makes it possible to start your diagnoses. Without this understanding, you are likely to treat all problems as "worker" problems. The result is you are likely to be wrong 94% of the time.

2. DIAGNOSING if it's Common or Special Cause. This process starts by exploring the root cause of the error or problem.

COMMON CAUSE	SPECIAL CAUSE
Happens often	Random event
Regular variation in results	Results stable most of the time
High variation in equipment	Equipment stable
High variation in raw materials	Raw materials stable
High variation in training	Training stable
High variation in process	Process has stable SOP

3. IF COMMON CAUSE. Identify root cause problem along with possible solutions. Common Cause problems often have multiple causes. However, there is usually one element that is the primary issue. In most cases, the cause will involve variation in equipment, methods, training, raw materials, or other elements of the system.

In a classic factory situation, identifying the root cause can often be done through control charting of variations in system inputs, equipment, work processes, and outputs. These types of charts allow you to quickly locate the biggest variation. The internet contains many free tools for control charting.

With "human systems," identifying variation can be more challenging because most systems that involve multiple humans as well as blended "human + smart software/equipment" systems often have huge variation in multiple areas. They have not been refined into Standardized Work Methods with written SOP documentation. Rather, they are a loose combination of elements made to work through the assumption that the humans will adapt and adjust. This approach is often successful when the system is new and run by those who created it. However, as the system scales and requires more/new people, problems increase.

To identify variation in "human systems," start by identifying areas that have a high probability of variation. The easiest next step is to have those involved in the system rate the variation they observe using a simple High, Medium, Low indication. This approach usually is all that's needed with human systems. You can also quantify human variation through specially designed surveys or observation systems.

Having identified areas of variation, the next step is to implement small and focused experiments to control variations one step at a time. After the change is implemented, you can quantify the impact. Then move to the next area of variation until you've achieved the required stability in your system.

4. IF SPECIAL CAUSE, Stop and Think First. Special Cause errors need to be thought through before taking action. In some cases, they could be random, one-off events, such as loss of electricity due to a lightning strike or a once-in-a-century snowstorm delaying deliveries. In other cases, it might be that employees unknowingly did something that caused a problem. In these cases, take time to listen and understand employee insights, observations, and questions surrounding the problem. We start here because there is a real possibility that you have misdiagnosed the problem. The worker who is "closest to the work" might identify things you missed. Having confirmed SPECIAL CAUSE, take appropriate action, which might mean doing nothing if, for example, it was caused by a freak snowstorm that was well beyond normal. Or it could include making your standardized work methods clearer (if, for example, employees misunderstood them) or provide training/retraining of workers.

5. MONITOR THE SUSTAINED IMPACT OF YOUR SOLUTION. When an intervention is implemented, it's common to see a positive short-term impact because of increased attention on the issue by employees. The real challenge is whether the improvement is sustained. Is it because you've made a true root cause improvement? If it isn't, then you need to go back and dig deeper to identify the root cause and solution.

WHY Problem-Solving of Common versus Special Cause Problems Works

This approach works because it partitions problems into Common and Special Cause with distinct actions. It reduces the chances of "searches for the guilty employee" that is demoralizing when the problem is a Common Cause error of the system. It also reduces the chances of our overreacting and creating needless bureaucracy that slows operations or increases costs and worker frustration.

Barriers to Problem-Solving of Common versus Special Cause Problems

Ignorance of the difference between common and special cause is, by far, the biggest barrier to this approach. If a manager has been taught that problem-solving involves "finding the guilty," there is low to no chance that Common Cause problems will be diagnosed.

The second barrier is that Common Cause problems require that the person responsible for the system takes responsibility for improving it. Instead of blaming the workers, the manager must take responsibility. For some managers, being responsible for system failures is difficult to accept because they feel they are being blamed for the failure. We coach managers to avoid the "Blame Game" for both workers and themselves. They are taught to think of systems as dynamic things that, because of variation, can go from in control to out of control. They are encouraged to focus their energy on finding and fixing root cause issues as opposed to searching for the guilty.

System Problem-Solving Examples Involving VARIATION

1. The First and Most Famous Deming System Problem-Solving Success in the US

This first story is the backstory of the success story at Nashua Corporation that Dr. Deming shared in the documentary *If Japan Can, Why Can't We?* That TV special is credited with sparking a system approach to building quality into operational systems.

I'm aware of the story because my father was Nashua's director of central engineering at the time and was responsible for leading the project with Dr. Deming's coaching support.

The project involved reducing cost of production for Nashua Corporation's carbonless paper production lines in their Merrimack, New Hampshire, production facility. Carbonless paper has a unique coating on each side. It's most often used for multi-sheet forms because it creates multiple copies without the need for carbon paper.

At the start of the project, as my father would explain, management's existing belief was that poor work by employees was the source of the higher-than-reasonable costs of production.

Instead of blaming the workers, my dad set out to measure (system) variation, including the raw material inputs, the equipment, standard operating procedures, and worker training for all three shifts.

He quickly found that the viscosity or thickness of the coating used to make carbonless paper varied from barrel to barrel. The machine operators had to adjust the machines up and down based on each barrel of coating. When it was thick, they had to turn down the amount of coating being put on the paper. When it was thin, they had to turn up the amount of coating laid down.

The variation in viscosity of the coating resulted in abnormally high out-of-specification carbonless paper that had to be scrapped, reducing production output and creating a need to spend money on 100% inspection of product quality to prevent customer complaints.

Having identified viscosity as the root cause of production quality problems, my father worked with the supplier of the coatings to reduce it. This simple change resulted in savings from one machine alone of nearly $4 million in today's dollars.

Most important to note is that the variation in raw material was out of the workers' control. They were doing their best trying to adapt to changes. However, no matter how hard they worked, each barrel of raw material they poured into the coating machine was a dice roll.

2. An Example of Chasing Down a Common Cause Problem That Is Elusive

As I start writing this paragraph, my embarrassment and frustration with this challenge comes back to me. At our distillery, we wasted six months of problem-solving because we didn't consider Common Cause variation as the root cause of our problem.

The problem we faced was the "fill level" of our Custom Bourbon bottles. When a consumer ordered their bottle, our system converted their recipe into commands that our WoodCraft bottling machine used to create a consumer's custom bottle.

The problem was that custom bottles didn't have the same fill height. One bottle's fill would be higher than the one before it and lower than the next one. The variation wasn't big—about a half-inch. However, it was enough to make customers feel they were cheated on the fill.

Given that our bottling machine was a new-to-the-world invention bringing together technologies that had never been used with alcohol before, we immediately assumed the problem was in our programming, pumps, tubing systems, and so on.

Despite our best efforts, we could not eliminate the fill height problem. Finally, we resorted to a work-around. We added a "nudge" button to the machine that allowed the operator to add more to the bottle. *Note:* This is a typical work-around that employees do when a problem is out of their control.

One Saturday morning as we were preparing to open the distillery for custom bourbon experiences, I was talking about the problem with Greg Carroll, the engineer who had recently joined us full-time after graduation with his master's degree. He had spent hours reducing variations in the machine itself. However, the problem remained.

For the hundredth time, we went through the machine piece by piece looking for what we were missing. As we talked it over, we started laughing at the craziness of the situation. As we laughed, we started throwing out crazy ideas for what the cause of our problem could be.

Suddenly a thought came to us. "What if the variation is in the bottles themselves?" In between making custom bottles that day, Greg started running experiments using the same exact volume (measured by weight) into bottles with different bottle mold numbers.

EUREKA! (Sorry, I just love saying that, especially when it's a real Eureka!). The bottles varied by a half-inch when filled with the exact same volume. THE VARIATION IN BOTTLE FILL WAS BECAUSE OF VARIATION IN THE BOTTLES THEMSELVES. This is because the bottles are made using molds that are just slightly different. This meant that no matter how much we improved the accuracy of the machine, there was no way to get to the same fill height with these bottles. Even worse, it also means that when we do our "nudge" approach we are likely overfilling bottles, thus increasing our costs. It's a small amount, but over tens of thousands of bottles it gets to be expensive.

Stupidly, rather than look at the obvious causes of our fill problem, we focused our blame/search on the bottling machine. This is a lesson that neither Greg nor I will ever forget.

In the end we discovered a simple solution to the bottle variation issue. We are looking into getting longer tamper-evident "shrinks" for the bottles, so the fill level is covered. EUREKA! Again!

3. Reducing Variation Increases Success

We installed a new high-speed bottling line at the distillery. The startup was going poorly. The line would break down, causing us to stop and make a fix every six minutes on average. It didn't help that sales of our Noble Oak and Dexter brands were skyrocketing. We felt pressure from our distribution partners to make, package, and ship 50% more volume than we had ever shipped in a month.

Our original bottling line was reliable, but it wasn't built to handle the new volume levels. The new bottling line was unreliable. The initial focus for the Brain Brew Crew, the machine vendor, and our collaboration partner was to focus on the number of cases shipped each week. Despite a clear focus on improving, the new line output did not meaningfully increase after months of work on the line.

Reflecting on the problem, I explored what Dr. Deming would do (Musical Chairs). I sketched out the system for how we were working to improve the output from the machine.

Suddenly I realized that, as a team, we were focused on the wrong metric: Cases shipped, the end consequence of improving the system. But that was too abstract for problem-solving. Our energy was scattered, leaping from working on one part of the machine to the other. Because the situation was urgent, sometimes we implemented multiple changes at the same time, making interpretation of learning challenging.

To sharpen our focus, we turned everyone's energy to reducing the number of breakdowns occurring each hour. We divided the machine into four modules—Module 1: Rinse and Fill, Module 2: Corking, Module 3: Labeling and Tamper-Evident Shrink, and Module 4: Case Packing. We charted the number and types of breakdowns in each module. Not surprisingly, every module had an unacceptable level of variation.

Kainon Loebker, the team leader, was enabled and empowered to set the direction. At the end of each day, he sent out the data on breakdowns, along with a written description of which changes had been made in each module and his hypotheses on what the team would do next to reduce breakdowns.

Kainon focused first on Module 2: Corking, realizing a meaningful improvement. This was celebrated, as the change proved to be a true, root cause fix. Next, he focused on Module 3: Labeling and Shrinks. Multiple cycles of problem-solving, including informal CREATE sessions, resulted in the number of breakdowns going from 10 an hour down to 4 an hour in two weeks. And before long, 1 or 2 breakdowns an hour were not unusual.

Most importantly, the team had a new hope that, after months of frustration, they now were on the path to having the machine working reliably. And, when future "special cause" problems occurred—cork vendor changed specs without our approval, a pump failed, a bottle gripper failed—the team was mentally ready and able to problem-solve and get the machine running again.

Final Observations on Problem-Solving Systems Improvements

The statement that 94% of problems are a result of common cause errors in the system may seem extreme. However, in the 47 years since my father first taught me this fact, I've come to believe that the number is not an exaggeration. In fact, in many organizations I've worked with, the system is the cause of more than 99% of the problems.

Recently, a senior vice president asked me when the system we were working on would be fixed and finished. My response was clear, direct, and probably a little louder and bolder than maybe it should have been:

NEVER!

So long as you have competitors with a passion for creating something new and better, you will never be able to stop improving.

- Trees that stop growing die.

- Oysters in New London Bay (visible through the window to my right as I type this) that stop growing die.

Dr. Deming famously challenged leaders to embrace "Never-Ending Improvement." The leadership of the Ford Motor Company believed that they sounded like it would take too long. They asked that it be changed to "Continuous Improvement."

Having thought about this for some time, I've concluded that what leadership, managers, and employees need to adopt is a mindset of:

NEVER-ENDING CONTINUOUS IMPROVEMENT

Insights for Managers of Proactive Employees

The PROACTIVE Problem Solving course teaches a simplified version of the Deming system for improving a system. It creates fast impacts with the smallest amount of studying and learning.

The course for managers provides a deeper dive into the full Deming system. This enables managers to guide their employees in more advanced methods for solving system problems.

For managers, here are some additional ideas to start teams problem-solving system challenges.

1. APPRECIATION FOR THE SYSTEM: As mentioned earlier, the first step is making the system around the problem area easy to see. The simple start is a system map, as described earlier. Helping your employees is important as they begin to see how the various system components work together to make the system successful. The next step is to define **(1)** The one overall mission of the system and the ONE metric that quantifies success; **(2)** Enabling metrics, these are metrics that are predictive of the ONE metric of the system, and **(3)** The key stakeholders who input into the system and receive the outputs of the system.

2. LEARN AND APPLY CONTROL CHARTING: Learning how to create and interpret a control chart will change your life forever for the good. It gives you a way to qualitatively identify Common and Special Cause errors. It also provides you with a quantitative feedback loop when you implement changes.

3. TAKE RESPONSIBILITY FOR COMMON CAUSE ERRORS: In a speech about Dr. Deming, my father said this about the need for managers and leaders to understand the differences between Special Cause and Common Cause.

The most important point to be made for the success of this Deming program is that no involvement of the system or any reduction of special causes of variation and trouble will take place unless management attacks common causes with as much science and vigor as the production workers and engineers attack special causes.

I'm not asking you to take the blame for errors of the system. Rather, I'm encouraging you to provide the energy, support, and resources needed to identify and reduce Common Cause errors.

PART THREE

Driving Out RISK as You Bring Your Idea to Life

CHAPTER 9

Plan-Do-Study-Act Cycles of Learning

DR. DEMING'S THEORY OF KNOWLEDGE is a mindset and method for learning. It's useful for solving problems, creating new learning, and neutralizing Death Threats. Recall, Death Threats are issues that could prevent your new idea from being successful. They involve anything from technical feasibility, cost of implementation, and safety issues to environmental concerns to fit with corporate strategy.

The method Deming used to enable his Theory of Knowledge is known as the Deming Cycle or, more specifically, the Plan-Do-Study-Act (PDSA) Cycles of Learning. As we discussed earlier, it's a variation of the scientific method that Dr. Deming taught the Japanese after World War II and the Western World in the 1980s.

Among students of Innovation Engineering, it's also known by the irreverent name Fail FAST Fail CHEAP (FFFC) cycles of learning.

The emphasis of PDSA/FFFC is on FAST and CHEAP. It's about finding ways to reduce risk of failure through fast and cheap experiments. Each cycle of PDSA builds confidence, courage, and sparks new ideas for how to solve the problem you face.

Simple PDSA

PDSA begins with clarity on WHAT you are trying to learn or problem-solve. It also includes clarity on how you will know if the learning has been accomplished and/or the problem solved. It then continues with four steps:

PLAN: Here you define what you will be doing (what experiment, test, learning effort, collaboration, etc.) to learn more or problem-solve. It also involves identifying what success looks like/when you will know it's time to stop. (Upon reaching "x" milestone, after running "x" number of trials, after "x" amount of time.)

DO: Here you carry out your plan and document what happened, including any data or observations.

STUDY: This details what you learned from your DO activity. Did you achieve the learning/problem-solving that was in your PLAN? Study is just as important when something works as when it doesn't. Understanding why something DIDN'T work will spark ideas for new PDSA cycles of learning. Understanding why something DID work will provide understanding on how to sustain your success.

ACT: This is a decision point based on what you've learned in STUDY about your DO relative to your PLAN. For big challenges, the answer is most often to repeat the cycle again with a different DO.

When your STUDY indicates you achieved your PLAN, then it's time to implement the new idea you have validated. Sometimes the right answer is to STOP the cycles and to archive the learning. I say archive because, if you are a 24/7 idea person, it is highly likely that sometime in the future—as new technologies and understandings occur—you might be able to reactivate this project.

The Secret to My Success in Life is Simple: Formal and Informal PDSAs

In a world that is overloaded with data, yet scarce in wisdom, PDSA really is a Theory of Knowledge, as Dr. Deming called it.

I've done PDSAs so many times I barely realize when I'm doing it. Without thinking, when faced with a challenge my mind automatically:

1) Imagines a hypothesis for solving the problem (PLAN).
2) Finds a way to try something to learn more (DO).
3) Confronts reality—on what worked and didn't work (STUDY).
4) Pivots, adapts, and repeats (ACT).

I find it useful to do both formal PDSA cycles and informal PDSA cycles. Formal cycles involve disciplined documentation of each step. This is invaluable when there are other people, departments, divisions, and/or companies involved. Formal cycles are also critical for historical documentation of corporate learning. The new breed of innovation project management platforms (such as the one Innovation Engineering Black Belts use) make it easy to borrow wisdom from projects across the organization when faced with similar Death Threats.

Informal PDSA cycles are valuable when the challenge is focused and doesn't involve many people. In my experience, sometimes informal PDSA cycles happen in such rapid succession that I find it most useful to just do them and then to sit down and summarize what I've learned. My primary place to record these PDSA learnings is a Moleskine pocket-size notebook. I've literally filled hundreds of these books over the years. In my case, I find writing down my thoughts and observations helps me think through my learning. I use Informal PDSA cycles in many ways. Here's a few very recent examples:

Quick Problem-Solving: When our snowplow wouldn't start one morning, I quickly did rapid PDSA cycles to find the issue. In this case, it was a loose battery cable under the driver's seat that had shaken loose and a dead battery.

Learning More: When we decided to franchise our WoodCraft Bourbon Blending experience, I did informal PDSA cycles with more than a dozen people with franchising expertise from franchise marketing companies to franchisors. My learning from these visits and calls was recorded in my Moleskine.

Resolving Death Threats: When preparing to make and serve cocktails at an opening reception at our daughter Victoria's destination wedding, I did disciplined learning cycles on what ingredients could be mixed ahead of time without impacting taste, what cocktails worked as both alcohol and nonalcohol versions, and serving speed. Again my Moleskine notebook became my reference library.

Why PDSA Works

PDSA works because it gives structure to your learnings. It challenges you to reexamine what you know or think you know. It forces you to embrace your ignorance and become comfortable with not knowing the answer to everything.

The use of emotionally charged language like "Death Threats" and "Killer Issues" is done for psychological reasons. All new ideas that are worth doing require change. And change ignites fear. This fear needs to be respected. Phrases such as "Death Threat" evokes the same emotional intensity that fear of change ignites.

By giving voice to our fears as "Death Threats," we are creating a displacement in our mind. At the extreme we basically move our mind from "Frozen in FEAR of change" to labeling the fear as a "Death Threat to be problem-solved."

By relabeling risks as "Death Threats," solving the problem becomes less personal. A personal attack of "Your idea won't work" is translated into the less personal, "There could be a Death Threat with your idea." This provides space for the problem finder and idea generator to collaborate and find ways to mitigate the potential Death Threat.

Barriers to PDSA

The biggest barrier to PDSA is not being fully engaged with solving the problem before you. Creating anything new is hard work. If you don't love it, you're never going to invest the energy required to create the starting ideas and to do the considerable problem-solving required to solve it.

When you are really passionate about solving a problem, a chain reaction of positives occurs:

YOU CONFRONT REALITY: You view project Death Threats as part of the process of turning your idea into reality. You view failed PDSA cycles as your pathway to success.

YOU TRANSFORM INSTEAD OF COMPROMISING: When dealing with Death Threats, you find a way to dissolve them without losing focus on your overall project mission. When you lack passion for solving a problem, you give up and compromise on your idea. Lacking a passionate advocate, the idea becomes a task to be completed, as opposed to a quest to make a meaningful difference.

YOU DON'T FEAR FAILURE: Your quest to vaporize the problem pulls you forward without worries about what other people think when a PDSA cycle fails. When an experiment fails, you simply use more PDSA cycles.

YOU AGGRESSIVELY CHANGE YOUR IDEA TO FULFILL YOUR MISSION: When solving a problem you are passionate about, you are very open to changing your idea as you learn what needs to be done to accomplish your mission. When you are not passionate, defending and protecting the idea as first stated is more important than achieving your mission.

Learning to let go of your original idea is an important skill to develop. With new ideas, it is inevitable that, at the start of an idea, you can't see the full pathway to making it reality. You have a hypothesis, for sure. However, as you get into the details, you will run into new and surprising Death Threats that will require you to adapt and adjust your idea.

Research finds that the average idea in large companies loses about 50% of the value it can deliver because of compromises. When an organization fully embraces the PDSA mindset instead of compromises, ideas increase in value on average by at least 26%.

Three Quick PDSA Examples

It's Great, but We Can't Afford It

A team at a food company had a major cost problem with one of their best-selling products. The product tasted great but had low profitability because the formula included a very expensive ingredient.

An employee at the company suggested using a similar yet lower-cost ingredient. After suggesting the idea, she was told that they'd considered changing but felt it wouldn't work. They had identified several "Death Threats": How would it impact taste? Would it be shelf-stable? Could their equipment produce products, as the new ingredient had a different viscosity?

After taking one of our classes, she became determined to do some PDSA cycles to dissolve the Death Threats.

She started by running lab-scale tests with the new ingredient to see if she could resolve the taste and stability issues. After about a dozen cycles, she proved that she could create the same taste in a stable format.

Having solved the taste and stability issues, she then focused her PDSA on finding a way to produce the product using the existing equipment.

Despite many experiments, nothing was working. She was close to giving up. At an update meeting, her problem-solving coach asked if there was another way to achieve the same flavor but using a different method. This set off a joint mind dump where they worked together to create a collection of possible options.

After about an hour, the project leader got an idea to apply the methods she discovered from her lab—scale work on taste to a third raw material that they knew worked with their equipment.

Quickly, the project leader did a PDSA cycle and YES, it worked! Combining her discoveries from the lab with this raw material created the flavor, stability, and manufacturability that was needed.

A Night Shift Invents Solution

The plant manager at a manufacturing company went through our Innovation Engineering training with his team leaders and some frontline workers.

About a month later, he called me to share the story of how his night shift team had faced a production problem. The production line had stopped because of a collection of what should have been random events all occurring at the same time. Classic methods for restarting the line were unsuccessful.

An hour of debate by the team resulted in endless loops of conversation that didn't result in ideas worth trying. Then someone suggested "using those problem-solving things."

They laughed and agreed it was worth a try. They wrote down the three most important production operations. They then did a Mind

Dump for ideas to try, things to adjust, or things to change for each of the three areas.

One of the employees then picked two ideas and said, "What would happen if we did this and this?" The group laughed, as the two options picked were contradictory. Despite this contradiction, they shared some ideas on what might happen and how they might change the ideas. They repeated the process with different people picking two or three things to think on.

In a half-hour, they had a collection of ideas to try. They ranked them based on ease of doing and their judgment on potential for success. They then executed PDSA cycles on the first and then the second. Eureka! The second solution worked, and the line was back in production.

Frozen Mystery Meats

Recently, my wife and I came to the realization that our two freezers were filled with mostly unknown, unmarked packages. Well, to be honest, those were the leftovers and other foods I'd placed into the freezer. The ones Debbie put in the freezer had clear dates and descriptions. While it was good to have the dates, it was also embarrassing how old the food was and how unlikely it was to still be edible.

During COVID I decided to cook our way to two totally empty freezers. When I first cooked our "vintage" frozen food, the taste was horrible. Rather than give up, I took making old frozen food edible as a problem to be solved. We mined the internet and texted friends for ideas and advice.

We adopted a system of experimentation. We would take out two foods at a time from the freezer for different PDSA experiments. This also gave us two chances to create something edible. Again, my trusty Moleskine documented our learning.

From our PDSA cycles we learned that some foods responded best to slow and gentle defrosting, some were better cooked direct from frozen, others were improved using sous vide (the frozen food being placed in a plastic bag in a hot water bath) to seal in juices, and still others were best if cooked with sauces and "mix ins" to improve flavor and texture.

Looking back, a key to our willingness to experiment was the fact that there seemed to be nothing to lose. The only alternative to experimentation was to throw the food away. And that just didn't feel right to us. Our intrinsic passion for not wasting food drove our willingness to run experiments, fail, learn, and find a new way of cooking them.

Final Thoughts on PDSA

The Innovation Engineering curriculum on campus has six college courses. A few years ago, the faculty on campus and at the Eureka! Ranch were together for dinner. Someone asked what is the ONE THING that, above all others, is the foundation of what we are teaching students, leaders, managers, and employees.

My mind bounced across our research and teachings. I thought of concepts such as the importance of curiosity, doing the math, stimulus, diversity, and driving out fear.

As we went around the table, these and others were mentioned with the supporting "logic" that is common when academics gather.

My son, Brad, who had completed the courses at the University of Maine and who now worked for the Ranch on the education team, said that for him the answer was PDSA. He felt that within PDSA lay all the other elements. With PDSA you need to have curiosity, it takes math to quantify learnings, it requires stimulus and diversity to implement experiments, and the process itself drives out fear.

Brad was right. PDSA is the core. It is how ideas become reality and, as Dr. Deming taught, how reliable knowledge is created.

The value of PDSA is reinforced when you understand the difference between the similar but very different—PDSA (Plan-Do-Study-Act) and PDCA (Plan-Do-Check-Act). They are both valuable but are not interchangeable. Deming was focused on PDSA as the means for discovering wisdom.

Whereas PDSA discovers new knowledge, PDCA is effective at implementing changes across a culture, department, or production facility.

We need PDSA to discover how we will win, improve, and change our team, our organization, and the world. We need PDCA to scale our new systems.

Insights for Managers of Proactive Employees

Developing trust among your employees for PDSA takes time and patience. It requires them to replace "declaring and defending" of their ideas with "imagine and learn." It means feeling psychologically safe enough to share hypotheses of ideas that may or may not work.

When helping others engage in PDSA, I often use questions like this:

Hypothesis

"What would be the ideal solution?"

"What's the easiest thing we could do to reduce the problem by 50%?"

Experiments

"How can we learn more?"

"What's the fastest and cheapest way to learn more?"

Other advice for managers when coaching PDSA includes:

1. DEATH THREATS CLUSTER INTO THREE AREAS: When reviewing a project, there are three types of Death Threats for you to consider and to teach your team about: **(1)** Technology Risk (Will the idea work?), **(2)** Market Risk (Will the idea sell to customers, management, or the organization as a whole?), and **(3)** Organizational Risk (Is the return worth the investment in time, energy, and money?).

2. SMALL STEPS BUILD MOMENTUM: When your team is first doing PDSA cycles, small steps can build their confidence. Robert Maurer, in his book *One Small Step Can Change Your Life, The Kaizen Way,* explained why small steps matter, "All changes, even positive ones, are scary. Attempts to reach goals through radical or revolutionary means often fail because they heighten fear. But the small steps of Kaizen disarm the brain's fear response, stimulating rational thought."

3. LEARNING CYCLES CAN DETERMINE IF A DEATH THREAT IS REAL: Your team has identified a Death Threat. Before they begin trying to neutralize it, have them do a PDSA cycle to confirm that the Death Threat is real. When an idea is Meaningfully Unique, it's common for people to overreact and think that something different is a Death Threat—when in truth it isn't.

4. TEACHING MOMENTS: There are many opportunities for "teaching moments" when coaching PDSA. For example, often employees will not see Death Threats because they have a limited field of view on how they impact other parts of the organization. You can use these moments to teach them how their work fits into the broader system. Another teaching moment is when they are reporting STUDY. The classic mindset is to report on tasks and task completion when talking about STUDY. You can use these moments to teach them how to report "What Did they Learn?" And even more specifically, why do they think the DO worked . . . or didn't work?

5. DIAGNOSING "NONCOMPLIANCE": You will inevitably run into situations where employees are unwilling to confront Death Threats or to follow the PDSA method. The root cause is usually either **(1)** They don't know what to do and need more training, 2) They are so busy with their work they don't have the time to do PDSA cycles, or **(3)** They don't feel the project mission is as important as other work. The first two causes can be addressed easily. The third is the most detrimental to success. The only thing you can do is to invest time explaining why the problem is very important.

CHAPTER 10

How Math Ignites Support and Drives Down Risk

DOING MATH ON YOUR IDEA'S POTENTIAL value and cost to execute can ignite pull for your idea within your team and organization.

Math includes estimates of the potential benefits from your idea in sales, profits, effectiveness, efficiency, safety, and or productivity. Math also includes estimates of the investment of time, energy, and/or money it will take to commercialize your idea.

You generate extra support and pull for your idea when the benefits it could deliver are significantly greater than the investment required.

For example, if your idea has an investment cost that is too high versus the potential return the idea could generate, it's probably not worth doing. If your idea will take months to implement, then another idea with faster impact might be the smarter choice.

I realize that for an "Idea Guru" to write that math is critical for problem-solving might seem contradictory to your stereotypical perception of creativity.

Embracing math early in the process of idea generation is a key reason that clients love working with the Eureka! Ranch team. Doing math early encourages teams to confront reality from the start, when ideas can be easily adapted and improved. It also creates a healthy balance of inspiration with practicality.

Math is so important that a mantra taught in our Innovation Engineering courses is "No Math No Project." The math we are talking about doesn't require complicated spreadsheets for financial analysis. All it takes is to confront the realities of the cost (in time, energy, and money) versus the potential benefits.

A recipe might be amazing, but the cost of the ingredients could be beyond your budget, or they might not be available in your local stores. Or an idea for arranging a carpool system for your child's soccer team might simply be more work than it's worth. Or an idea for a new computer system at your company to solve a problem might not be worth the investment.

How To Do Math Early in the Process

The most common excuse for not doing math early in the problem-solving process is that there are lots of uncertainties. This thinking is fueled by a misconception that math that is not precise and accurate is not worth doing. The truth is the process of doing the math, even with rough estimates, deepens your thinking regarding your idea and its potential consequences.

The challenge when estimating math for a truly Meaningfully Unique idea is the lack of directly comparable reference points for doing estimates.

To do the math early, when there is high uncertainty, the method we use and teach is called Fermi Estimating. It's named after the famous scientist Enrico Fermi, who was known to be outstanding at doing "back of the envelope" estimates of the math associated with experiments.

Fermi Estimating is a three-step process:

STEP 1: Deconstruct your challenge into a few factors you can estimate.

STEP 2: Estimate each factor and document your thinking.

STEP 3: Do the simple math to estimate your number.

For example, assume that our Death Threat for our nonprofit fundraising event is, "Will this idea for an event generate the profits we need to raise?"

Fermi Estimating gives us a method for estimating, before we've committed to the event, how much we might raise for our non-profit. The process begins with defining the potential sources of income: 1) event sponsorship revenue, 2) ticket sales, 3) concession sales, and, 4) if appropriate, availability of government grants. We then deconstruct each source into elements we can estimate. For ticket sales we might estimate 20 VIP tables @ $750 each and then 100 individual tickets @ $50 each. We then do the same for the other sources of income. We then do estimates of our costs for all major expenses. Lastly, we subtract expenses from revenue to have a first estimate of our potential profit from the event.

Your first estimate shifts your thinking to a broader perspective. It's common that seeing the reality of early estimates will spark ideas for how to make the idea more attractive. In the case of our fund-raiser, these might be ideas for increasing revenue and/or decreasing costs.

The same type of estimating can be done on a small process improvement idea when the primary variable is the amount of employee time it takes to do the current process versus an estimate for the new method.

Using Fermi Math to Drive Down Risk

It's likely that you will have varying levels of confidence in the numbers that make up your first estimate. This variation is a benefit. It provides clarity on where to focus your problem-solving. Basically, areas with high uncertainty are the factors that could cause your idea to fail. In simple terms, the process works like this.

STEP 1: *Create a "Best Case" forecast.* For each input, use estimates that you feel there is only a one-in-five chance that the actual number is higher than your estimate.

STEP 2: *Create a "Worst Case" forecast.* In this case, estimate where there is only a one-in-five chance that the actual number is below your estimate.

STEP 3: *Compare the two forecasts.* Focus on the estimates for each input. Look for those inputs that are the farthest apart. The larger the variation between the numbers, the greater the uncertainty and potential for this input to be a source of risk to the idea's success.

STEP 4: *Run PDSA cycles to reduce variation and drive down risk.* Start with the inputs with the greatest variation. PDSA cycles might range from gathering more data, running a simulation to estimate labor requirements, checking regulatory constraints, or doing a survey of staff to quantify the number of times a specific costly event is encountered.

With our Brain Brew Distillery, this process focuses our team's energy during our development process. It provides clarity and focus to our PDSA cycles. Step by step, we run PDSA cycles on input after input. With each cycle, changes are made in our idea. Most of the time this results in ideas becoming stronger and stronger. Sometimes the PDSA cycles uncover bigger challenges that can't be solved, resulting in the idea being stopped and archived. When this happens, I teach the team that stopping an idea is disappointing, but it is the right thing to do. Stopping an idea for a good reason is a win for the organization. The key is to be open, transparent, and honest with the process.

Why Fermi Math Works

The "back of the envelope" math of Fermi Estimating works because it is rare that new ideas fail by 1%, 2%, 5%, or even 10%. Most ideas that are Meaningfully Unique succeed or fail by a large margin, since the math and assumptions were likely faulty from the start.

Fermi Math gives us a way to bring a reality check to our idea. A very loose "this idea will work better" or "this idea will reduce cost" is replaced with an estimate that says we could work x% faster or at y% lower cost.

Having even a rough estimate gives you a sense of the magnitude of the potential for the idea. Knowing the potential for the idea balances out our natural tendency to only see the "cost" of the idea in time, energy, and money associated with a change in how we work.

When you see the cost AND the benefit, then you have the knowledge to make a smarter decision on the pursuit of an idea. For example, if an idea will take you about two hours to do, but it will save you 30 minutes a week for a year, it's worth doing. Conversely, if an idea will cost $1,000 to implement but will only save $10 a month, it's hard to justify.

Barriers to Fermi Math

A false sense of precision is the biggest barrier to Fermi Math. In school we were taught that there is a right and wrong answer to every math problem. In the real world, all numbers have variation. And a collection of numbers with variation multiplied together amplify that variation.

Interestingly, it is those who are most comfortable with math who often have the biggest challenge with Fermi math. It's common that their sense of self-worth has been built around their ability to get the correct answer to math problems. When asked to do a rough estimate, sometimes just to an "order of magnitude," they become anxious. Their fear of getting the wrong answer gets in the way of learning more about the potential for the project.

"Math experts" need to replace their quest for precision with a search for learning. They need to accept uncertainty and variation as fundamental to new ideas and, frankly, life. It helps if they embrace the more advanced version of Fermi estimating, where estimates of variation are used to focus PDSA cycles.

Doing the math at the end of a project is too late to help you make smarter decisions. The most valuable place to do math is at the start. And then again and again during the project to help focus your development efforts on decreasing risk and thus increasing odds of success.

Someone who is very resistant to doing the math on an idea is a red flag for me. More often than not, I've found that the root cause of resistance to math is a fear that the math won't work. Sometimes this fear is grounded, sometimes it's not. Either way, avoiding the reality of the situation is not useful.

Doing the math is not a judgment of you or your ideas. Rather, it's a reality check that is best done early and often to guide where you invest your energy. Math is about confronting the reality of your situation to aid your accomplishment of your project.

The importance of confronting reality and being honest with yourself when creating was articulated by the author Ernest Hemingway:

> *The most essential gift for a good writer is a built-in, shockproof shit detector. This is the writer's radar and all great writers have had it.*
>
> —Ernest Hemingway

Examples of Fermi Math

Setting Priorities on a Collection of Ideas for Reducing Health Care Costs

A hospital group was looking for ideas for how to reduce health care costs. They published a Blue Card articulating the need for ideas. They engaged frontline employees to create an abundance of Yellow Cards. They then sorted the ideas into two groups. The largest group were CORE Ideas that could be led and done by frontline staff. A smaller but still significant group of ideas were identified as LEAP Ideas. These would require significant investment of time, staff, and money to develop and activate.

The first step was to empower managers of frontline staff to work with their teams to do the CORE ideas.

The second step was to activate a team to do the math on the LEAP ideas. When needed, they ran quick PDSA cycles to create their first forecasts of execution costs and potential cost savings.

After doing the math, they quickly learned that their first instincts on potential for net savings (after cost to execute) did not match their Fermi estimates. This was because of the number of variables that made up costs and savings. Sometimes new technologies resulted in huge savings. Other times they didn't. Some simple ideas saved a little for each shift on each hospital ward. However, the little savings became large when calculated over all shifts and all wards.

Ideas were sorted into three sets. The first set of ideas made up a first wave of projects to be executed. The second set of ideas were set up for a second wave to be executed in about six months. The third set of ideas were archived for future investigation. Some of these ideas required more work. Others would be easier to execute after ideas from first and second waves were worked on.

"Math is Boring, and No One Cares"

I've been a host on two network television shows and a radio show. My role on the shows was to give entrepreneurs, inventors, and businesspeople ideas and advice on their ideas.

As the ABC *American Inventor* television show started filming, I would often do some quick Fermi math on the potential for success, as well as costs and profitability. I'd give a simplified overview of that math as justification for why the idea might not work.

My Fermi math was not popular with the show's producers. After a couple of days of filming, I was told, "Stop doing the math. Math is boring, and no one cares. Just tell them if the idea will work or not. And try to make it funny."

Because I believe so deeply in the value of doing the math, I pivoted my comments. Instead of talking specifics, I spoke of "high risk versus low potential reward" or "the idea definitely seems worth the effort."

Yes, I kept doing the math because, frankly, it's the only way I know to evaluate the potential for an idea. Quite simply, ideas without math run the risk of being fantasies with little-to-no chance of achieving a positive return versus the investment required to make them real. Alternatively, ideas that offer the potential for WOW benefit relative to investment deserve to be celebrated and encouraged.

Faster Fermi Math Saves Us Over 50%

Joe and I were at a trade show for distilled spirits. On the last day of the show, Joe pulled me aside and said that one of the exhibitors had a piece of equipment that he used at trade shows he wanted to get rid of because there was a new version coming out. He was willing to sell it to us for less than half the normal price if we would say yes today and load it in our van.

The piece of equipment was not something we were looking for. However, Joe felt that, if we reconfigured one of our bottling lines, it could help us increase production and thus reduce our cost per case.

I responded, "Let's do the math." And thus we pulled some chairs up to an empty table, took out some paper and our phones as calculators. We did Fermi estimates of what impact the change would make. We had to do multiple estimates because a production line is an interconnected system of pieces of equipment that must work together.

In about 20 minutes we estimated our best guess, worst case and best case. We then double-checked our numbers. The answer was obvious: BUY IT! And we did. The equipment paid for itself in just two months.

This scene of us doing fast Fermi math is repeated regularly. In fact, we did it the other night on the phone. Joe had just visited a potential franchisee for our WoodCraft Custom Bourbon offering. The company he met with has a different twist on how they would like to implement our technologies. Working together on the phone, we did the math to evaluate the opportunity. Within five minutes, we were both really excited about the potential.

It is much easier for us to do the math and make decisions, as we are both comfortable estimating math. And, as the two people who lead our small company (CEO and President), we have the full authority to make decisions.

Our ability to instantly take quick action based on math gives us a competitive edge. Importantly, those who work for us are taught to use math to make decisions on what we call their "sphere of influence." They might not be making decisions on capital investments, but they are making decisions on ideas that drive never-ending, continuous improvement of how they work. For low-risk decisions, they JUST DO. For higher risk decisions, they share their math and Yellow Card with their manager, and for highest risk they turn to Joe and me.

Final Thoughts on Fermi Math

With PROACTIVE Problem Solving, math is **(1)** A way to find out if an idea is worth doing, **(2)** A method for focusing a team on decreasing risk, and **(3)** A method for communicating ideas.

In my mind, math as a communication tool is another important reason why it's worth developing the capability and confidence to do math across your culture. The Yellow Card defines your idea in words. Fermi math defines your idea as a series of numbers that interact with each other to evaluate an improvement. When you have the math—even really rough and ugly math—you then begin to understand what you need to do and change to make your idea successful.

The older I get, the less firm I've become in most of my beliefs. I've learned that what is true today is likely to be replaced by new truths in the future as technologies, work systems, and marketplace conditions change.

One thing that hasn't changed in more than 50 years is the belief that "No Math No Project." My father first taught me the importance of estimating math when I started my first business producing and selling learn-to-juggle kits. He sat me at the kitchen table and had me do the math on my expenses and potential revenue. It worked. I made some money and reinvested it in other ideas. It's a process I have continued for more than a half-century and taught to the people I manage.

Insights for Managers of Proactive Employees

1. REDUCE MATH ANXIETY BY FOCUSING ON THINKING. Math as taught in school is polarizing. For many, it is something they dread, as the focus is on getting the right answer. With Fermi estimating, the focus is more on the thinking than on the numbers. The math is a way to communicate what we think is possible with our idea. By translating the focus to the thinking instead of numeric precision, stress is often reduced. Another way to help employees do math is to provide them with a chart of standardized values on elements of operations that they might need.

2. MONTE CARLO SIMULATION: The most advanced form of Fermi Estimating is when you input your best case and worst case numbers into what is called a Monte Carlo simulation. Named after the famous Monte Carlo casino, it's a system for doing multiple simulations to help you understand your probability of success. The classic approach takes the variation in your forecast and does some 10,000 simulations. The process transforms your uncertainty about each input in your estimate into a probability distribution. It shows you the odds of achieving various outcomes. There are numerous software programs that can do the math for you. Our Innovation Engineering internet portal includes a model that anyone can use, even without extensive math training or experience. What I particularly like about our model is that it automatically identifies the variables that have the greatest variation, so you instantly know where to focus your PDSA energies.

3. THE THREE LEVELS OF ESTIMATES. When you move forward with your project, the variation in your forecast should decrease as you learn more. The three classic levels of increasing precision with estimates include:

A. *Fermi Estimating.* This begins with a simple point estimate as outlined above. The next step is to do a probability estimate to understand uncertainty. This can involve comparing worst case versus best case estimates. Or it can be a full Monte Carlo probability estimate.

B. *PDSA Calibration of Estimates:* Calibration involves comparing your estimate versus numbers from other projects or previous experiences. Comparing against points of reference is often very helpful in reducing variation in your estimate inputs. It's not uncommon to have to adjust up or down because the calibration data is not 100% comparable. If you are really passionate about calibration, it's worth learning and using Delphi forecasting, a validated method for mining wisdom from a collection of experts. You can learn more about it by searching on the internet. We feel it's such an important tool that we built an automated and very easy-to-use version of Delphi that is included in our Innovation Engineering Internet portal of tools.

C. *PDSA Experimentation:* PDSA Experimentation uses cycles of learning to confirm and improve estimates. Often the experiments are on a smaller scale or on a focused portion of your idea. For example, if your idea involves human labor, you might set up the actions required and time it takes to do the new tasks. You can then compare that timing versus the current approach.

CHAPTER 11

Making It Real: Prototyping and Project Acceleration

PROTOTYPING IDEAS in even the roughest of forms is useful in driving down risk and discovering ideas for improving your idea.

We use Prototyping as part of PDSA cycles of learning.

We also use Prototyping as part of IE CREATE Sessions to spark ideas. In this case, Prototyping ignites new and unexpected thinking by tactically engaging participants in creating solutions to the problem being worked on.

Prototyping involves translating your problem into physical elements that can be felt, touched, and, yes, even played with. The tactile/physical representation of the parts and pieces that make up your challenge are mixed, matched, assembled, and reassembled in multiple ways. This inevitably leads to the discovery of new and unexpected solutions.

Not only is Prototyping amazingly productive, it's also a ton of fun. There is something magical that happens to the human mind when it receives tactile stimulus in its full, three-dimensional glory.

The downside to Prototyping is it can take some time, energy, and sometimes a little money to activate it. However, IE students on and off campus are convinced the ideas that Prototyping delivers are well worth the required investment.

The following is a quick example of one of the many ways to do Prototyping. It's a class assignment in one of the IE courses. In this class, students are challenged to invent a new type of wallet. It can't be a digital wallet. It must be a physical thing. They first create a collection of wallet ideas through methods such as Mind Dump.

Next, they are challenged to make real one or more of their wallet ideas. To assist their Prototyping, a table is provided, filled with materials for constructing representations of their wallet ideas. Examples of materials include: fabric, cardboard, elastics, tape, cord, leather, bags, balls, scissors, pipe cleaners, twist ties, metal, wood, aluminum foil, and a multitude of other things that could provide inspiration/wallet-building material.

Their effort then moves to physically creating a representation of one or more of their ideas. Participants are always amazed by the number of new problems and ideas that are generated as they work to create their original idea. When you are physically touching the materials, you gain insights and ideas that were invisible to your mental representation. Nearly every team ends up creating an idea that is bigger and better than the one they started with.

If you've never experienced something like this, it's likely that you might assume it's a childish waste of time. I can relate to that feeling. Over the years, when I'm tired and worn out, I often ask myself is it worth searching for and gathering the materials for Prototyping. Inevitably, my team and I do it. And every time we say afterward that we are glad we did.

Simple Prototyping

There are three types of prototypes:

- **Concept Prototypes** "look like" the real thing but don't function.
- **Functional Prototypes** "work like" the real thing but are often ugly.
- **Real Thing Prototypes** "look like and work like" the real thing.

Here are some very simple examples:

Say you are doing a home repair. Gather raw materials that could be part of the solution. My dad had a box that contained hundreds of different screws, bolts, hooks, parts, and pieces. When working on something, he'd sort through it, trying one part and then another. In this collection of what some would call junk, he inevitably found a solution.

The same approach can be used when cooking. Simply pull out the ingredients and look at them on the counter. Then start thinking substitutions, twists, and adjustments you could make to create a very special and unique recipe. By the way, this is what chefs do when they walk food markets looking for which vegetables, fruits, fish, and meats are available that look particularly great. From this collection they often create a set of specials that their restaurant will offer that night.

When the Eureka! Ranch team creates food products or drinks, we'll often pull together the raw ingredients and potential substitute ingredients in a big pile. This allows participants to play with creating new versions. We'll also go from a different direction and give participants modeling clay and decorations to allow them to create a physical representation of what a new product could look like.

Other examples of Prototyping projects we've done over the years include:

When working on a system for serving cocktail flights at the distillery, I went to the workshop with some barrel staves and various glasses. An hour later we had a first generation that we tried. Then a second generation that was better. Then a final design that we scaled.

When working on weed killers, we literally "planted weeds" in weird pots and locations and then used various equipment to treat the weeds.

When creating ideas for rust-prevention paint, we gathered junk chairs, tables, and grills and had participants go about preparing and restoring them.

When creating ideas for an amusement park, we gave participants the welcome materials and asked them to plan a day for a family of five, each with different interests.

When working on a data entry system, you might print out screen shots of your database, showing how users will go from one screen to the next.

Use Prototyping when working on a system or service problem. In today's world there are 10,000x more problems with work systems and services than with products. In these cases, we create a representation of the system or services. These might be index cards with process steps on them that you pin to a bulletin board or post as sticky notes on a wall.

Each element can be shifted, sorted, and reorganized. You can also add sub-notes to each stating the EFFECT or FUNCTION each provides. This approach can spark ideas for alternative and better ways to deliver the same FUNCTION in a more effective or efficient way.

Often photos from Homeward Trail are printed out and used to represent Magic Moments in the system or service.

For example, if we were working on ideas for improving the flow of raw materials through our department at our factory, we might take photos of the paperwork, the containers, the storage space. These photos allow us to step back and think about the flow, sparking new ideas.

When we were designing the physical space of our first WoodCraft Bourbon Blender franchise location, Joe drew the space with chalk on the floor of our distillery. He then had the team walk through the workflow to find opportunities for improvement.

Why Prototyping Works

At the most basic level, Prototyping helps others see your idea as you perceive it. It also makes it easier for others to offer helpful improvements to your idea.

There is also academic evidence that hands-on engagement engages the brain at a deeper level than simply observing the process.

When we are physically touching, sorting, and combining, new ideas are created that wouldn't occur otherwise. Imagining making a dessert is very different from touching and feeling the process of creating the dessert in person.

It could be that when the pieces are laid out before us we don't have to hold them in our memory as tightly, thus freeing up our minds to look more deeply at interconnections and alternatives.

There is also often an element of surprise when you are trying to assemble something. The parts just don't fit or align as your mind thought they would. This creates a problem that the mind immediately seeks to solve.

Finally, there is a natural aspect of play that comes with the physical nature of the process. This relaxes the brain and opens it to new ideas.

Barriers to Prototyping

The biggest barrier to Prototyping is the anxiety associated with making something that looks good and works well.

Years ago, shop and home economics classes taught young people cooking, woodworking, metalworking, and so on. Today, with the rise of our digital world, these hands-on classes have been mostly discontinued. A professor of engineering told me that, over the last 10 to 20 years, she's seen a continuing decline in the hands-on skills and confidence in lab classes.

Fortunately, every adult was at one time a child who enjoyed making things, from sandcastles to imaginary toy villages. The best way I've found to reactivate hands-on engagement is by encouraging people to just do it. Gather the materials they might need to make it easy for them and just start the process.

To build their confidence, I will often do something foolish. I'll create something outlandish, funky, or ugly. The laughter reduces anxiety associated with making something perfect and pretty.

Three More Examples of Prototyping

Crystal Pepsi—Breaking It into Pieces

Many years ago, the Pepsi Cola company was looking for new ideas for its Pepsi brand. We spent weeks exploring and creating. I felt the ideas we had created were good but not great, so on a Saturday afternoon I challenged myself to think of something bigger and bolder.

I lined up cans and bottles of Pepsi and Diet Pepsi alongside many of the raw ingredients that made up these products. I played with things. I mixed in some of this, a little of that, and some things from my kitchen that had never been in a Pepsi before and, frankly, never should be.

I opened the cans and bottles, listening, smelling, feeling the sounds and smells. I stirred, shook, and even sprayed the Pepsi.

As is typical, the first 30 minutes were fun and filled with new sensations. Then as I ran out of things to try—and no big ideas showed up—I got bored. I knew from experience that I was now near the point where ideas often show up. Once the "obvious" ideas are used up—the "bored brain" starts making nonobvious connections.

I read the label on the can and the ingredient list.

I stirred in crazy stuff. Tasted and spit out most.

The more I played, the more I kept coming back to the ingredient list. I had most of the ingredients in front of me. Those I didn't have I wrote on index cards. Desperate for a new idea, I started, one at a time, taking each ingredient out of the set. I then forced myself to describe the new Pepsi both without the ingredient and with a substitution for the ingredient.

I took out sugar and substituted Maple Syrup or Honey. Holding aside the technical challenges and cost of each—I tried it. It was OK, but not a WOW.

I took out the caramel coloring and thought what it would be like.

Hmmmm . . . looking at the sticky caramel coloring, I thought what impact it might have on the Pepsi if it wasn't there. I forced myself to stop thinking like a chemical engineer and to think more innocently.

An idea popped into my head: "If we took out the caramel we could have a Pepsi that was more refreshing because it didn't have the sticky caramel aftertaste." Now this was very interesting.

What would it be called?

I grabbed a bottle of 7-Up and poured it into a glass with ice. I then stood up and talked the idea out loud. For some reason I've always found that, when my ear hears an idea, it's very different than simply reading it or speaking it to myself without verbalizing.

I showed the caramel and how sticky it was—explaining that because we took it out this Pepsi (holding up the 7-Up glass) was more refreshing. We call it . . . I waited for my brain to think of the name . . . I waited some more . . . It's called "Crystal Pepsi" . . . the more refreshing cola because it has no sticky caramel aftertaste.

We created a drawing of a package with a short explanation and added it to the batch of ideas going out on Monday for testing with consumers. When the test results came in, Crystal Pepsi was the highest scoring idea in the set and of hundreds of various ideas we'd created and tested for Pepsi over the previous three years.

The idea for Crystal Pepsi was simple. However, within the company, there were many twists and turns. The idea of a more refreshing Crystal Pepsi was seen as potentially damaging to the parent Pepsi brand. As a result, Crystal Pepsi was transformed from more refreshing to a 7-Up cola clone—no color, no caffeine.

Test market results were very strong. However, the positioning of "more refreshing Pepsi" was politically challenging for the organization. Therefore, when the product was introduced at the Super Bowl the next year, it was transformed into a different idea. "More refreshing because of no sticky caramel" became "you've never seen a Pepsi like this—no caffeine, no color." It ended up being a huge flop. However, it continues to make a reappearance every few years.

As with many of my innovation adventures, there is much more to this story that is best shared over a dram of our Dexter bourbon.

A Prototype to Reduce Risks with a New Information System

A company made hundreds of different products. The problem they had was keeping track of the specifications, approvals, ordering of materials, and so on. It was very painful.

A team had created a new system for handling the flow of information. To test it, we gathered everyone involved in the system and created a virtual prototype.

We set up tables in a long row with different stakeholders seated in the order that they see the information. We gave them a quick training on the new system and work process. Then we simulated the system by sending papers for new products into the start of the system. The papers were handed from department to department, with each department adding information (or a summary of what they would add) to each sheet.

As you'd expect, we quickly ran into a "bug" in our virtual system. We had missing data. To fix it, we stopped the line, learned about the mistake, and changed our system. Then we started again.

It took almost two days to get the system running properly in our virtual paper-and-pencil way.

We then programmed the new system and again gathered the stakeholders, this time for a day, each with laptops in front of them. This time the system didn't have nearly as many breakdowns. Because the core system was working, we were able to gather ideas and advice from the participants about how to make our system even more efficient and effective.

Implementation of the new system required some changes to software as well as training. For a system of this complexity, we anticipated that fixing the system would take 18 to 24 months. However, by enabling those close to the work—visualizing the system—and working together, it was up and running in six months.

The biggest benefit of Prototyping a new system is the empowerment of those who work with it. When something doesn't work as intended, instead of griping about it, they tell someone, and it gets fixed.

Medical Devices and Ocean-Based Oil Drilling Platforms

You wouldn't think that doctors who are expert surgeons could invent ideas by playing with Lincoln Logs, Erector construction sets, pipe cleaners, Popsicle sticks, duct tape, and stuffed animals.

However, that's exactly what happened one afternoon at the Eureka! Ranch. A high-end medical company was looking for ideas for new types of surgical instruments. A group of expert surgeons came together to create ideas for designing tools that can help surgeons save the time it takes to do specific operations.

Methods like Mind Dump, Lawbreaker, Matrix, and so on were used during the morning. Starting in the afternoon, Prototyping was introduced. The doctors did not take well to the concept, at first. In fact, some overtly resisted.

With a big smile, we just got started. We took a surgical challenge and assumed that one of the stuffed animals had that medical issue. Then we went to a giant table that was filled with raw materials to build something that would simulate that medical device.

Soon the doctors went from skeptics to zealots—building, trying, changing until they had something that just might work. Many of the ideas were nonobvious leaps, making them eligible for patent filing.

In a similar situation, a company that made anchoring systems for ocean oil-drilling platforms needed new ideas for more rapidly anchoring platforms to the seabed. The anchoring of an oil platform is very expensive and dangerous. The faster it's done, the less it costs both the oil company and the rigging company.

Like the doctors, in the afternoon we challenged them to create new systems for anchoring these mammoth oil rigs out on the high seas. They were instructed to use the collection of wood, tape, pulleys, and rope to build a model of a platform and a prototype of new ideas for anchoring it.

It took about 45 minutes to get them engaged. However, just as with the doctors, soon they were excitedly playing with different solutions. And just as with medical devices, patentable ideas got invented.

Final Thoughts on Prototyping

I continue to be amazed at how effective Prototyping is. Something magical happens when idea challenges are translated into tangible prototypes or representations of the challenge.

Yes, it takes time and work to create the experience. However, it's always worth it. Even some time later, people will recall ideas and insights they gained in the experience.

Just do it!

Project Acceleration—A System for Accelerating Change

PDSA provides a method to make change happen within organizations. It gives employees a safe and effective way to explore, develop, and activate meaningful solutions to the problems they face.

PDSA helps individuals activate their PROACTIVE solutions. In the case of an individual, the focus is usually within their sphere of influence.

Kevin Cahill, executive director of the Deming Institute, explained the concept of sphere of influence and how he used methods such as PDSA to activate his career despite not having the support of his manager:

> *I know my grandfather said quality starts in the boardroom, and I've heard many people say unless you're at the top, it's not worth doing. I disagree, because you're not always going to get the person at the top right off the bat.* ***I believe that every single person, in every single organization, has some sphere of influence they can impact.***
>
> *Ultimately, that's what I did. When I started working, just out of college, I had leaders who were fantastic people, but they really didn't want to change, because what they were doing at that time was working well.*
>
> *I started out as an assistant to an assistant. But I realized that I could use my grandfather's ideas and thinking to improve the areas that I had some influence over. In time, it had a real impact and people started noticing that this guy did something really interesting and different. What it enabled me to do was to move up in the organization. Eventually those who are willing to learn the new way of thinking and applying it could end up being in charge of that leader who is unwilling to learn or to change.*
>
> —Kevin Cahill,
> Executive Director, Deming Institute

Activating change among a group of people—a team, department, division, or organization—is often stressful for leaders. While they logically want to activate PROACTIVE changes in how employees work, they often feel anxiety when urging employees to make changes.

PDSA provides a disciplined and documented method for managing change. Blue and Yellow cards make it easy to communicate what is being done and why.

Project acceleration of PROACTIVE Problem Solving can be activated by adopting a set of roles and meeting rhythms for helping employees be PROACTIVE.

The heart of project acceleration is an employee-coaching system that consists of three roles:

1. PROJECT LEADER: This is the person who leads the project to find, develop, and implement solutions to a problem. It was inspired by how Procter & Gamble brand managers and Toyota chief engineers work. In simple terms, the project leader is the person who integrates the work of other project stakeholders such as departments, experts, and sometimes even suppliers or customers. The project leader's job is to translate the requirements of each stakeholder into an idea that delivers against the Blue Card mission for the project. They have responsibility for the project but no authority over the stakeholders. To accomplish their mission, they need to run many rapid PDSA cycles to ensure the system delivers on the mission without being compromised.

2. MANAGEMENT COACH: Management coaches help guide the project leaders in the execution of the project and work to ensure organizational alignment with the project. They do this by helping them understand the broader issues that the employee likely doesn't understand. They also provide perspective on the risk/reward equation that is part of all new ideas. Lastly, they often provide ideas and help with getting the attention and support of those from whom the project leader needs help.

3. PROCESS COACH: Process coaches are primarily teachers. They reinforce the training the project leader has participated in. They are also experts in accelerating PDSA cycles of learning. They are usually IE Black Belts. Their training gives them an understanding of a broad range of tools and techniques that can help the project leader work smarter and faster.

The management and process coaches' primary responsibilities are to be honest and helpful.

Honest means when they see a problem with the project, they say something. This total honesty policy ensures that project leaders don't waste their time chasing an idea that has critical Death Threats or that is not aligned with organizational strategies or mission.

Helpful means that they give ideas and advice for how to improve, problem-solve, and accelerate PDSA cycles.

Having these three roles is the ideal. However, when you are first starting out with PROACTIVE Problem Solving, it is not uncommon for project leaders to work by themselves within their "sphere of influence."

When projects are pursued that are outside of an individual's sphere, it is helpful to add a management coach (the employee's manager) and/or a process coach (the organization's trainers/IE Black Belts).

The driver of PDSA success is cycle time. For some organizations and in some situations, the cycle time for PDSA learning cycles is weekly. When the challenge is urgent or a high business priority, it's not uncommon to have meetings to review PDSA a few times a week if not daily.

The fastest PDSA cycle time I've experienced was when we were first inventing WoodCraft Finishing technology. Each PDSA cycle took about an hour. In total, we completed 72 cycles during a seven-day sprint.

At each PDSA meeting, the project leader reports on the Study and Act portions of the cycles that were agreed to at the previous meeting. At the start, it's common to work just one PDSA cycle. As confidence grows, project leaders concurrently work two to five PDSA cycles at the same time.

Insights for Managers of Proactive Employees

1. JUST DO IT—COMMIT TIME FOR COACHING: Coaching those who work for you does three things. It helps them: **(1)** Solve their immediate challenge, **(2)** Build confidence in their ability to think through challenges, and **(3)** Activate their engagement on more challenges. When you give time to coaching you will also realize an intrinsic return on your investment. The reward you will feel helping develop and enable PROACTIVE Problem Solving with your team members is priceless.

2. JUST ARCHIVE IT: As PROACTIVE Problem Solving is activated, there will be projects that are just not moving forward. In many cases, project leaders miss meetings or don't find the time to work their PDSA cycles. The root cause is usually either they don't know what to do or they don't believe in the project. In the case of not knowing what to do, your job as coach is to give them an easy first step for working their PDSA. In the case where they don't believe in the project, explain again why it's important. If the project leader still doesn't see it as important, then archive the project. A project leader who doesn't have intrinsic motivation will never invest the time and energy to do the necessary PDSA cycles to make the idea successful.

3. ADVANCED RESEARCH TOOLS: There are many methods that can help accelerate the process. For example, Paired Comparison research compares the current work system versus a new proposed system. It gives you quantitative feedback on how those working in the system perceive the new approach. Problem Surveys can help you quantify the size and frequency of the problem you are working on. Idea Starter surveys can help you sort a collection of potential solutions to find the one that the stakeholders perceive to have the highest potential. Delphi research can help you mine for wisdom and forecast the future based on the conscious and subconscious wisdom of subject matter experts inside and outside your organization. All these research methods can be activated with free research tools available on the internet.

Advice to Leaders

BILL CONWAY WAS A VISIONARY CEO of Nashua Corporation. He was the first Fortune 500 CEO to embrace Dr. Deming's system thinking. My father worked for Bill as director of Central Engineering. My friend Tim Hogan set up a meeting for me with Bill about a year before he passed away.

I intended to summarize my meeting, but when I read my original summary, I could feel again Bill's tremendous impact. Thus, I've included the notes in full, with a few notes to help readers connect the dots to PROACTIVE Problem Solving.

First Impression—ABSOLUTE CONVICTION

The first impression from Bill is an aura of ABSOLUTE CONVICTION. Even at age 84, his absolute belief is clear and persuasive. He told me that this belief was critical for success. Deming advised Bill that, as CEO, it was his job to make the company commitment. Bill explained to his company staff, "This (Deming Continuous Improvement) is not a consensus decision. We are going to commit to it, commit to changing how we work. You are going to do it, or you will not be working here."

Talking with Bill, you get the impression that quality is not a task or a job: It's a religion, and he believes in that religion with his heart and soul. Nothing is more important. He recalled that on one of Dr. Deming's visits he told him he would miss a morning meeting with him because of a previously booked appointment. Dr. Deming scolded him: "You don't have anything more important to do." Bill canceled his appointment.

Success Principle #1: Working on the Right Things

Bill explained that the first role of leadership is to make sure everyone is working on the right things. I explained that many companies are currently focused on cutting costs because their offerings were perceived by customers as commodities. Bill's response was clear and direct: "Then they are not working on the right things. They have to stop working on reducing cost and start working on innovation." I explained that it was hard to convince them. His response was clear, firm, and direct: "Then they're stupid."

Hearing an 84-year-old man say "Then they're stupid" in a loud and firm voice was a bit shocking, even if it was true. I gently challenged him on his directness. He went on to explain that Dr. Deming was very impatient and sorrowful. Sorrowful that he was unable to save every company. Sorrowful that he could not get through to every leader. Impatient to get to those who he could convert, as companies in the early 1980s were dying very fast. Bill said they would explain the importance of focusing on quality/continuous improvement twice, and if the leader didn't get it (and I quote Bill directly) "then to hell with them." Many CEOs felt insulted by his and Dr. Deming's directness (or rudely honest words). However, given their absolute conviction, they moved on, without regrets, to those who were willing to learn and apply.

> **DOUG NOTE:** *Blue Cards that set the WHAT and WHY were inspired in part by Bill's comments on Working on the Right Things.*

Success Principle #2: Leaders Getting Close to the Work

Bill was very clear that one of the big problems with most companies is that the leadership has become separated from the real work of the company. They don't fully understand the reality of the challenges that workers face. He advocates leaders spending time on the front lines to learn the work. "The bosses need to get close to the work," he said. "The work of sales. The work of manufacturing. The work of R&D. They need to fully understand the causes of the workers' challenges." They can only do this when they SEE, FEEL, TOUCH, and EXPERIENCE the REAL WORK. You cannot get it from meetings, reports, or PowerPoint presentations. This is reminiscent of Deming's variation of his frequently stated message that *94% of the problems are due to management because only management can change the system.*

DOUG NOTE: *Stimulus Mining provides a structure for doing this without stress.*

Success Principle #3: Offer Amnesty and Admit Failure

When the leadership learns a new process, flaws in past decisions are often revealed. Bill found that it was effective to offer amnesty and forgiveness for all past mistakes. He also encouraged the CEO to take responsibility for the past failures. CEOs were advised to say, "I am the problem because I am responsible for the company's systems, and I am working to change."

DOUG NOTE: *Leaders and managers are often reluctant to admit mistakes. They shouldn't be. I've observed the power of being honest with employees multiple times. The result is always greater respect and support from employees.*

Success Principle #4: Target CEOs and Points of Light

The primary marketing system for spreading the Deming mindset was to talk directly to CEOs. They needed to have a serious conversation about the reality of the economics and challenges of the marketplace. Messages that CEOs found persuasive included growing profitability, increasing job security, and making the company a more fun place to work. One way they would bring the benefit of continuous improvement to life was by asking, "How would you like to have fewer things to keep you awake at night?"

The secondary marketing approach was through people in organizations that Bill called "points of light." These are people down in the organization who have read Deming's books, seen the TV stories (such as *If Japan Can, Why Can't We*?), or heard about the program from a friend. They are eager learners. They are passionate about studying and taking action on quality/continuous improvement.

DOUG NOTE: *This insight led us to adopting a "Diffusion of Innovation" approach to changing a culture. Rather than forcing everyone to engage at one time, we find it more valuable to first* *activate employees who are innovators or early adopters. These pioneers pull the rest of the organization into the new mindset.*

Success Principle #5: Don't Waste Time on "Dippers" and "Oxygen Eaters"

"The world is filled with people who waste your time," Bill said. The urgency of getting to those who are ready and willing to take action caused Dr. Deming and Bill to be relentless in avoiding two types of time wasters. He defined "dippers" as those who come to the Deming training so that they can say, "I've been dipped." They talk a lot and never take action. He defined "oxygen eaters" as those who want to hold long conversations about the virtues of the program, asking for details, references, case studies, and so on as ways to delay taking action. They seem like they're interested, but in truth they are not. When meeting with executives about the power of System Thinking, Dr. Deming and Bill found that executives either got it or they didn't. Given Deming's age at the time (in his mid-80s to early 90s), he had a deep sense of urgency that drove them to move on to those who got it. When people didn't get it, he and Bill were sorrowful but took an attitude of "to hell with them."

DOUG NOTE: *Similarly, some people seem to have a Plan, Plan, Plan, Plan, and never a DO mindset. A sense of urgency to take action among all levels of the organization is critical to building a culture of PROACTIVE Problem Solving.*

The One Big Mistake They Made

"Given how obvious and commonsense our message was, we thought that the change would be easy," Bill explained. "Looking back, it's clear that we didn't comprehend how difficult change was going to be. The leaders needed much more training and support than they thought they did and than we thought they did. It is such a change they can't absorb it in the multi-day training. They need more help." If Bill was to do it all again he would provide more teaching of the tools, application of the tools, support systems, and coaching. Dr. Deming spent weeks each year teaching him all day, every day, through every breakfast, lunch, and dinner. Bill explained that the core message to leaders should be: "Your job is to learn more, get smarter, and to help others get smarter."

DOUG NOTE: *The Eureka! Ranch and Brain Brew teams have learned this repeatedly. This learning is what drives Never-Ending Continuous Improvement of all our systems.*

Closing Challenge from Bill:

I asked Bill what advice he had for us as we embarked on the journey to create an innovation/PROACTIVE Problem-Solving revolution. He put his hand on my shoulder, looked me straight in the eye, and said, "You must do it. America needs it now. The country is failing because bosses are not doing the right things. Do it now. Do it faster. Have no tolerance for excuses."

Bottom Line: In the 1980s, the need was Quality. Today the need is problem-solving to STOP THE STUPID, as well as innovation of Disruptive and Meaningfully Unique strategies, offerings, and business models.

Closing Thoughts

If you would not be forgotten, as soon as you are dead and rotten, either write things worth reading, or do things worth the writing.

—Ben Franklin

YOUR MISSION is to take what you've learned on these pages and to "do things worth the writing."

Founding Father Ben Franklin was a PROACTIVE Problem Solver. His curiosity led him to do a PDSA experiment flying a kite in a thunderstorm. From this he discovered electricity. He also applied what he learned to the development of lightning rods to save houses from fire.

Franklin was someone who loved to "Stop the Stupid." When he saw something that was stupid, he did something about it. Frustrated with what he was supposed to do as the American Colonies' representative to England and later to France, he pioneered systems for how America's ambassadors should work. Frustrated with high shelves at his newly renovated home in Philadelphia, he invented a tool to help him get books down from a high shelf. Frustrated with the smoke from his wood stove in the winter months, he invented the Franklin Stove.

Unshakable Belief Is How You Change Your Culture: Scientists at Rensselaer Polytechnic Institute have found that when just 10% of the population holds an UNSHAKABLE belief, their belief will always be adopted by most of the society. They explain, "When the number of committed opinion holders is below 10%, there is no visible progress in the spread of ideas. It would literally take the amount of time comparable to the age of the universe for this size group to reach the majority."

The Rensselaer findings are encouraging. It means that it only takes a few people to create the momentum needed to create a culture of PROACTIVE Problem Solving. As a manager, your mission is to first build Unshakable Belief within yourself. Then build the same belief within your team.

I'm going to end this book with two quotes selected to encourage you to "do things worth the writing."

The first one is thought to be from author Mark Twain. However, recent research doubts this fact. Either way, it's a great thought . . .

> *Twenty years from now you will be more disappointed by the things you didn't do than by the ones you did do. So throw off the bowlines! Sail away from safe harbor. Catch the trade winds in your sails. Explore. Dream. Discover!*

The second is the quote from Ben Franklin that I end all my books, lectures, and trainings with. It's how I lead my life and how I challenge you to lead yours.

> *Up Sluggard And Waste Not Life*
> *In The Grave Will Be Sleeping Enough*
>
> —Benjamin Franklin

So what are you waiting for?

Get Up! Get Out! And Get Going!

Where to Learn More

EUREKA! RANCH
Innovation consulting and training
EurekaRanch.com

EUREKA! EUROPE
Services in the UK and Europe
Eureka1Europe.com

INNOVATION ENGINEERING
Curriculum and university courses
InnovationEngineering.org

DOUG HALL
Beach Bar Blog, keynote lectures, trainings, and books
DougHall.com

BRAIN BREW DISTILLERY
Products, collaborations, and technology licensing
BrainBrewWhiskey.com

DOUG BOOKS & PAPERS

Jump Start Your Brain—A freewheeling adventure ride on unlocking your creativity.

Making the Courage Connection—For those looking for inspiration to get up get out and get going.

Jump Start Your Business Brain—A classic on creating and communicating your idea. Named multiple times to the list of Top 100 business books of all time.

Jump Start Your Marketing Brain (2005)—The bible on the science of how to persuade and sell to others.

North Pole Tenderfoot—A very funny story that will inspire your spirit of adventure!

Jump Start Your Brain 2.0—A rewritten, updated, and improved version of the classic.

Driving Eureka! (2019)—A review of the Innovation Engineering Curriculum.

PROACTIVE Problem Solving (2024)—The Organizational Engagement System Behind the World's Most Disruptive Bourbon Distillery.

Kahle, L. R., D. B. Hall, and M. J. Kosinski. (1997) "The Real-Time Response Survey in New Product Research: It's About Time." *Journal of Consumer Marketing,* 14:3 (1997).

Hall, D.B., (2010) "The New Art and Science of Leading Innovation," *League of Innovation in Community Colleges Innovations Conference,* New York City, NY.

Hall, D.B., (2018) *Cycles to Mastery a New Way of Teaching System Driven Innovation,* Deming Institute Conference, Manhattan Beach California, USA.

APA Handbook of Consumer Psychology (2022)—Authored chapter on Innovation and Product Development.

Books by Other Authors That I've Found to be Invaluable

Out of the Crises and *The New Economics*—W. Edwards Deming—The OG of system thinking. If I was in charge of required books for schools, they would both be on my list.

The Whole Brain Business Book—Ann Herrmann-Nehdi—The epic masterwork on understanding how to turbocharge your whole brain.

Diffusion of Innovations—Everett M. Rogers—The bible on how change happens across teams, departments, divisions, organizations, and cultures.

Principles of Forecasting—J. Scott Armstrong—The ultimate book on how to use math to forecast the success of your ideas.

The New Craft of the Cocktail—Dale DeGroff—Everything you need to know about cocktails.

Where is Doug From?

As a Canadian American, I live in two worlds—Springbrook, Prince Edward Island, Canada, and Cincinnati, Ohio, USA. PEI is a rural island where conversations often begin with understanding "where you are from"—your dad, your mother's maiden name, etc. It's part of connecting at a deeper level.

To provide the same understanding on the roots of this book—here's a short summary of where I and the learnings shared on these pages come from.

My career as an innovator started in 1971 at age 12 when I invested the money I'd earned shoveling driveways in Nashua, New Hampshire, into the production and marketing of learn-to-juggle kits. Profit from the kits was invested in additional entrepreneurial adventures performing as a magician/juggler and inventor of everything from new board games to toys and entertainment events.

Studying and graduating with a degree in chemical engineering at the University of Maine taught me how things work from a mechanical, electrical, and chemical perspective.

My combination of engineering skills and innovation experiences landed me a job at Procter & Gamble, first as an engineer at their Mehoopany Paper Mill, then in brand management at the company headquarters on 6th Street in Cincinnati. Over 10 years I went up through the ranks as brand manager, associate advertising manager, and eventually as leader of the P&G Invention Team.

Working with my kindred spirit Eric Schulz, we invented and shipped a record nine innovations for P&G brands in a 12-month period. Our success wasn't because we were smarter. Rather, it was because we focused on creating systems that enabled us to work faster and smarter.

After 10 years, I retired as an "employee" and founded what is known today as the Eureka! Ranch, an innovation consulting and training company.

Multiple television appearances and books later, I found myself wondering why some Eureka! Inventing sessions were more productive than others. Working with three statisticians, I embarked on two research projects.

The first study focused on the creation of ideas. It included surveys every 45 minutes as teams from Nike, Walt Disney, American Express, Procter & Gamble, Pepsi-Cola, and others came to Eureka! Ranch to invent big ideas. We measured them before, during, and after each project. From this analysis we discovered how Stimulus, Diversity, and Driving Out Fear impacted project success.

The second study focused on what made ideas successful in the marketplace. Here we studied quantitative data on more than 20,000 ideas from the Eureka! Ranch archives and the database of AcuPOLL, a market research company I founded and eventually sold. From this analysis, we discovered how to quantify Meaningful Uniqueness as well as how to improve how ideas are communicated.

The studies were supplemented with real-world research on more than $20 billion in active improvement projects in our Innovation Engineering portal and a literature review of more than 2,000 academic articles.

This research led to more books and articles. It also resulted in me being recognized with honorary doctorates from the University of Maine and the University of Prince Edward Island.

The research gave birth to a new field of academic study and management science and business leadership known as Innovation

Engineering. The core Innovation Engineering curriculum involves nine college courses of content and leads to associate degrees, graduate certificates and Blue and Black Belt certifications by the Innovation Engineering Institute.

A few years ago—with amazing support from my high school sweetheart and wife of many years—I started doing experiments on how wood interacts with whiskey. This work led to the creation of Brain Brew Custom WHISKeY and WoodCraft Bourbon Blender Franchising with my cofounder Joe Girgash. Leading the whiskey business through rapid growth caused me to rethink the importance of PROACTIVE Problem Solving. And thus, early one winter morning, the idea for this book was born. My goal is to use what I've learned from more than 50 years of innovation to build organizational engagement and, as a result, enable everyone to think smarter, faster, and more creatively.

Index